Tony Curtis, born in Dublin, 1955. He has published three collections of poetry, including *This Far North* (Dedalus, 1994). A further collection, *Three Songs of Home*, has been completed and will be published in 1998.

Dennis O'Driscoll, born in Tipperary, 1954. His fourth collection, *Quality Time* (Anvil), appeared in 1997. He writes on poetry for *Harvard Review*, *Poetry Review* and the *TLS*, as well as for Irish publications.

Tom Mathews, born in Dublin, 1952. He works there as a cartoonist, painter, critic and poet.

AS THE POET SAID...

Edited by Tony Curtis
From Dennis O'Driscoll's
"Pickings and Choosings" column
in *Poetry Ireland Review*

Cover and illustrations by Tom Mathews

Poetry Ireland / Éigse Éireann

First published in 1997
by Poetry Ireland Ltd./Éigse Éireann Teo.
Dublin Castle, Dublin 2, Ireland

with the assistance of The Arts Council / An Chomhairle Ealaíon
and the Arts Council of Northern Ireland.

Typeset by Kieran Nolan
Printed in Ireland by Colour Books Ltd.

ISBN   1–902121–00–7

Distribution

Ireland and world, with exception of Britain:
Poetry Ireland, Dublin Castle, Dublin 2.
Tel (+353 1) 671 4634, Fax (+353 1) 671 4634
e-mail poetry@iol.ie

Britain:
The Poetry Society, 22 Betterton Street, London WC2H 9BU
Tel (+44 171) 240 4810, Fax (+44 171) 240 4818
e-mail poetrysoc@dial.pipex.com

— Introduction —

In the spring of last year I was asked by Theo Dorgan, Director of Poetry Ireland, if I would like to edit a selection from Dennis O'Driscoll's "Pickings & Choosings" column for a special fiftieth edition of *Poetry Ireland Review*. The poet Michael Longley was to be the guest editor. My task was simply to cast an eye over Dennis's "Pickings & Choosings" and choose an entertaining selection that gave a flavour of the whole: a small flourish of fireworks to close the special fiftieth issue of the *Review*. The column had been an integral part of *Poetry Ireland Review* since *P.I.R. 20* (1987) and sadly with *P.I.R. 49* (1996) Dennis had decided to bring the lights down. It was therefore timely that a small edited selection should appear in *P.I.R. 50*. I accepted Theo's offer. Over the next few weeks I read, hacked and polished until I finally emerged into the daylight with what was to me a wonderful, but all too brief, selection. This was published with Dennis's blessing and Michael Longley's goodwill.

What I found in editing the column was that Dennis O'Driscoll had, over the years, compiled an intriguing body of work: a work that, in the world of poetry, played a small but not insignificant role. Every art needs someone listening to its murmurs: someone to remind us what's in the wind; through his "Pickings" column, Dennis had assiduously been doing this for years.

When taken out and dusted off the "Pickings" amounted to over two thousand quotes, from the obscure, the great and the good. It would appear that every poet has a different idea of what poetry is, where it springs from, what it means to them and its significance in the world. Some, as you will see, judge it to be the essence of life, while others see it as peripheral, if not entirely futile. I felt that all these differing voices, all these differing opinions, were simply too interesting to be placed back in the dark; hence my pleasure on being asked to expand the selection into this book.

I have no idea what kind of book Dennis imagined would emerge from my editing, but I had anticipated that when everything was washed, ironed and sorted we would have a light, funny book on our hands. However, I soon realised that I was looking at an entirely different beast. What began to emerge was a debate. It was as if I was listening to poets, scholars and critics conversing on poetry, like the Greeks of old. These arguments were intriguing as they explored, contradicted, even breached the bounds of common sense — saying the unsayable. Of course, for the listener this is marvellous. For those who think they are in the know, it is an awakening; for those who come to this debate feeling they do not know, it is an illumination.

In trying to put some order on the accumulated body of work certain themes began to emerge... 42 of them, to be precise. This, I was later informed, was the famous answer to "The Ultimate Question of Life, the Universe and Everything" in Douglas Adams's book *The Hitch Hiker's Guide to the Galaxy*. So perhaps there is some kind of symbiotic relationship between poetry and that elusive answer. I for one wouldn't be at all surprised if there was.

I would like to thank all the contributors from far and wide. A special word of thanks to Dennis O'Driscoll for his dedication to the compiler's art; he has supplied further quotations, collected since *P.I.R. 49*, to update this compilation. Finally, I would like to thank everyone in Poetry Ireland for their help. Long life to them all and to you.

Tony Curtis

August 1997
Dublin

Contents:

As the poet said

Poets on Poets:

"If one is not brave enough to speak one's mind, one should not be a poet."
— Tony Harrison, *The Observer*

"All people talk to themselves. Some are overheard and they are the poets."
— R.S. Thomas, *The South Bank Show*

"Anything that gets poets to *say* less seems like a worthy project."
— Peter Sirr, *Irish Literary Supplement*

"The poet is set against the world because he cannot accept that what there seems to be is all that there is."
— Ben Okri, *The Times*

"An artist is a bit of a scientist. They want to know the rules, the laws by which it all works."
— Les Murray, *The South Bank Show*

"The word 'poet' is a noun that sheds off adjectives."
— Seamus Heaney, *BBC 1*

"The adjective *neglected* may be applied to practically *any* poet from the past, even from the recent past."
— Richard Tillinghast, *The Gettysburg Review*

"A real poet doesn't draw attention to the fact he's a poet. The reason a poet is a poet is to write poems, not to advertise himself as a poet."
— Yehuda Amichai, *The Paris Review*

"A poet shouldn't be viewed through any prism other than that of his poems."
— Joseph Brodsky, *Partisan Review*

"A poet doesn't exist. Only poetry exists. It's what gets written down on the page or read from the stage that matters."
— Gerald Dawe, *RTE Radio 1*

"I don't know if I can analyse why poets are bad news; but in theory I think it would be much better to stick to accountants and solicitors."
— Wendy Cope, *BBC 2*

"Shakespeare had his problems, as did Alexander Pope. Authors do well to remember that they are not really kin to priests and politicians but to singers and stand-up comedians — entertainers of a devious sort."
— John Updike, *Vogue*

"Ever since Stephen Dedalus, poets have tended to look at themselves as if they were angels on loan from heaven, instead of scruffy old bolloxes going around the place looking for a bit of inspiration."
— Brendan Kennelly, *The Big Issues*

"Poets are almost human."
— Eiléan Ní Chuilleanáin, *Ropes*

"Bureaucrats and bus passengers respond with a touch of incredulity and alarm when they find out that they're dealing with a poet."
— Wislawa Szymborska, *Nobel Lecture*

"It's not one of the lucky times. There's a lot of bad poetry, bad poets, bad critics and bad readers."
— Thomas Kinsella, *The Irish Times*

"I think the great enemy of art is the ego. It keeps getting in the way. One needs the ego to disappear so that I become you; I become the people walking up and down the street."
— Paul Durcan, *Oxford Poetry*

"Poets are almost human."
— Eiléan Ní Chuilleanáin, *Ropes*

"The poet is essentially a medium. You take poetry from the people and then give it back to them."
— Micheal O'Siadhail, *The Irish Times*

"Poets are just craftsmen, there's nothing special about them."
— George Mackay Brown, *Catholic Herald*

"I believe that technique is important. I think that if most people who called themselves poets were tightrope-walkers they'd be dead."
— Michael Longley, *Fortnight*

Poetry is:

"Poetry is memory become image, and image become voice."
— Octavio Paz, *New York Times*

"Poetry is either language lit up by life or life lit up by language."
— Peter Porter, *BBC Radio 3*

"Poetry is a fire, well banked-down that it may warm survivors in the even-colder nights to come."
— Hugh Maxton, *Dedalus Irish Poets*

"Poetry is the most encompassing of the arts."
— Thomas McCarthy, *RTE Radio 1*

"Poetry is the culture thinking aloud, its consciousness."
— Roger Garfitt, *Poetry Review*

"Poetry is heart language."
— Fr. Michael Ruddy, *The Sunday Press*

"Poetry is language at its most nourishing. It's the breast milk of language."
— Robert Crawford, *The South Bank Show*

"Poetry is... the alcohol content of any given piece of literature."
— Grey Gowrie, *The Daily Telegraph*

"Poetry is language in orbit."
— Seamus Heaney, *Sunday Independent*

"Poetry is the purest of the language arts. It's the tightest cage, and if you can get it to sing in that cage it's really really wonderful."
— Rita Dove, *Poetry Flash*

"Poetry... is born of speech and silence. So it is a form of music."
— Paul Durcan, *In Dublin*

"Poetry, like traditional music, is a product of, and a repayment to, community."
— Bernard O'Donoghue, *PBS Bulletin*

"Poetry is a dividend from what you know and what you are."
— Czeslaw Milosz, *Poets & Writers*

"Poetry is an attempt to rescue what matters of one's life."
— Alan Ross, *BBC Radio 4*

"Poetry is always an attempt to hold what we love a little longer."
— Mark Doty, *BBC Radio 3*

"Poetry is a battle against the prompter, which can only give us someone else's lines to say. The poet has to speak his own lines, be in his own play."
— Craig Raine, *Gown*

"Poetry is a thief that comes in the middle of a new day, while the critics are still studying by night light."
— James Liddy, *Éire-Ireland*

"Poetry is written out of the need one has to write it. There is a void in oneself that echoes the Void without."
— Louis Simpson, *The Hudson Review*

"Poetry is an incurably semantic art and you can't really help it. You have to make sense."
— Joseph Brodsky, *American Poetry Review*

"Poetry is the art of using words charged with their utmost meaning."
— Dana Gioia, *The Atlantic*

"Poetry is language that sounds better and means more..."
— Charles Wright, *Quarter Notes*

As the poet said

"Poetry is a way of talking about things that frighten you."
— Mick Imlah, *The Daily Telegraph*

"Poetry's a zoo in which you keep demons and angels."
— Les Murray, *The Australian*

"Poetry is a tremendous school of insecurity and uncertainty. You never know whether what you've done is any good, still less whether you'll be able to do anything good tomorrow."
— Joseph Brodsky, *The New Yorker*

"Poetry is the closest literary form we have to silence."
— Marianne Boruch, *The Southern Review*

"Poetry is like a substance, the words stick together as though they were magnetized to each other."
— David Gascoyne, *Stand*

"Poetry is not a trade; it's an art, an extremely difficult art. It's a rare person, in my book, that can write a poem."
— Sebastian Barry, *The Irish Times*

"Poetry is not a fiefdom or a private domain. It is a city whose gates stand wide; which has never exactly welcomed its newcomers but has always found room for them."
— Eavan Boland, *Ronald Duncan Lecture*

"Poetry is the oldest form of written expression apart from household accounts."
— Julia Casterton, *Margin*

"Poetry... is a hotline to the emotions."
— Andrew Motion, *The Times*

"Poetry is the microwave oven of the arts."
— Robert Hanks, *The Independent*

"Poetry is there in a crisis, the power cut, the sudden bereavement, the dictatorship."
— Ruth Padel, *The Independent*

"... poetry is conservative (with a small and decidedly non-political 'c') in that it is defending eternal pleasures and truths. To participate in an art that is devoted to such verities — even in a minor way — is an immense privilege, and a serious responsibility."
— Douglas Dunn, *The Poet's Voice and Craft*

"Poetry is the art of saying in two words what is better said in ten."
— Brian Sewell, *Evening Standard*

"Poetry is old, as old as time; it is poverty, little books that fall apart, pub basements. Poets used to be mad or bad; now they're mostly just sad."
— Alan Jenkins, *Independent on Sunday*

"Poetry is utterly futile."
— Peter Reading, *The Times*

As the poet said

On the Craft:

"The thing about writing is that, if you have the impulse, you will find the time."
— Seamus Heaney, *RTE 1*

"I hate everything about writing except doing it."
— Tony Harrison, *The Independent*

"It's good practice to write as regularly as you can, even if that means having to tip the dustbin men a bit more at Christmas."
— Peter Sansom, *Writing Poems*

"The way to learn to write poetry is: to write poetry. So we pass directly from the aspiration to the activity itself."
— James Fenton, *Oxford University Gazette*

"Those who want to write good poems should be reading good poetry, not how-to books. Indeed, every fine poem *is* a how-to manual."
— Billy Collins, *Poets & Writers*

"A poet takes language, condenses it, charges it with energy, gives it a bit of oomph — and there's the poem!"
— Julie O'Callaghan, *RTE Radio 1*

"There's nothing like a punch in the mouth to remind you that that poem about your next-door neighbour was not as clever as you thought."
— Simon Armitage, *BBC Radio 4*

"What's writing really about? It's trying to take fuller possession of the reality of your life."
— Ted Hughes, *Independent on Sunday*

"Writing poetry is like trying to catch a black cat in a dark room."
— Robert Greacen, *The Irish Times Poetry Prize acceptance speech*

"Writing poems is like waiting for lightning to strike. But it's hard to order your life around that."
— Stephen Dobyns, *Publishers Weekly*

"Unless a poem surprises you a little bit, some little gate is opened by the words within themselves, then the poem could be perfectly okay, but it won't hold you forever."
— Seamus Heaney, *The Sunday Times*

"I'm reluctant to begin work on a poem unless I have the title, the first line and the last, or at least a clear idea of what they should contain. I suppose I've been brought up to believe in that triumvirate as the holy trinity of a poem, around which everything else must congregate."
— Simon Armitage, *How Poets Work*

"There must be three things in combination, I suggest, before the poetry can happen: soul, song and formal necessity."
— Derek Mahon, introducing *The Desert Route*

"Most writers of verse have several different personalities. The ideal is to find a style or a method that includes them all."
— Ted Hughes, *BBC Radio 4*

"The more of a poet that gets into their poems the better."
— Wendy Cope, *BBC Radio 3*

"My greatest fear is that I'll discover — or, worse, that someone else will point out to me — that I've stolen another man's words, thinking them my own."
— Thom Gunn, *The Economist*

"Human failings may be forgivable, but if lack of compassion, meanness of spirit, envy or cowardice are present in the poet's nature they will be evident in his verse. You cannot fake anything if you are trying to write serious poetry."
— Elizabeth Jennings, *The Independent*

"When a poem doesn't work, the first question to ask yourself is 'Am I telling the truth?'"
— Wendy Cope, *BBC Radio 3*

"My own sense of putting together a selection of poetry is to avoid perfection, not to necessarily edit out some of the weaker or goofier stuff, because that has some interesting merit of its own."
— Gary Snyder, *Poets & Writers*

"In every book there is a poem that belongs to the last one."
— Eiléan Ní Chuilleanáin, *The Canadian Journal of Irish Studies*

"There comes a point where I'll write a poem which I realise is the first of the next book, and then the new collection is complete."
— Michael Longley, *Books Ireland*

"Poets who write for children have a tricky job. The harder they try, the bigger they fail."
— Julie O'Callaghan, *The Irish Times*

"We learned from him that poetry, like charity, begins at home; that if you enjoy a vivid inner life and are alert to people and places, your home ground may prove to be a gold mine."
— Michael Longley, on John Hewitt, *The Irish Times*

"One of the hardest things about writing poetry is the way that experience can seem to exist only as material to end up in a poem."
— Michael O'Neill, *London Magazine*

"The ability to write poetry can be withdrawn as easily as it is given. To be suddenly empty of poetry is a frightening thought, like an abandonment."
— Helen Dunmore, *PBS Bulletin*

"Every poem is a sort of fit of desperation how to end it."
— Hugo Williams, *PBS Bulletin*

"Poetry builds up in your mind like a charge. If you go in too early, you'll muck it up, if you go in too late it'll be dry... At the right moment, the poem doesn't have words. It's a pressure."
— Les Murray, *The Australian*

"Poetry springs from a level below meaning; it is a molecular thing, a pattern of sound and image."
— Nuala Ní Dhomhnaill, *RTE 1*

"Words come, well ordered, the fluent vowels, the strong consonants binding the poem together. All seems to be well... And then, just when the end seems to be in sight, just when it is time to deliver the final hammer-stroke, something goes wrong, the poem falls to pieces in your hands. Or you know, beyond a doubt, the shape of it is wrong. Reluctantly, you throw it on the scrap heap."
— George Mackay Brown, *The Masked Fisherman*

"Poems come out of wonder, not out of knowing."
— Lucille Clifton, *Poets & Writers*

"It's just the continuous practice of verse that creates poetry."
— Derek Walcott, *American Poetry Review*

"Poetry may be the one activity where practice doesn't make perfect."
— Peter Dale, *Agenda*

Now, What Should I Write About?

"The selection of subject-matter is a primary artistic act."
— Thomas McCarthy, *RTE Radio 1*

"It is misguided to praise poets for their subjects. Many of them, like Walcott, had little choice in the matter. What poets do with their inheritances means everything."
— Paul Gray, *Time*

"The command which is unspoken but deep in the mystery of poetry is to somehow abdicate from audience, from self-promotion or self-alignment, and to go towards the subject, to give yourself over and disappear."
— Seamus Heaney, *RTE Radio 1*

"Self-expression is no reason for writing. The task is to make a work of art and, in doing so, to say something. Pity for poets who have no subject save themselves."
— Christopher Logue, *PBS Bulletin*

"It amazes me that there are still people around who would censor poets for their choice of subject-matter. There is no such thing as 'correct' subject-matter."
— Thomas McCarthy, *The Irish Review*

"While poetry can be many things, it is not a mere turning loose of the contents of one's head."
— Andrew Waterman, *London Magazine*

"I believe that poetry, no matter what its subject, should have some kind of entertainment value."
— Douglas Livingstone, *BBC Radio 3*

"There are no poetic subjects, only subjects to which we pay the right kind of attention."
— Marge Piercy, *Independent on Sunday*

"It is often preferable to take your subjects from life or even from newspapers... than to construct mysterious fantasies at one remove from reality. There's always enough to write about; indeed, there's too much."
— Gavin Ewart, *The Guardian*

"It takes several conditions to allow for great poetry. Apart from innate gifts and the opportunity to make something of them, a subject matter of wide relevance has to be at hand."
— Alfred Corn, *Poetry*

"Poetry will wither on the vine if you don't regularly come back to the simplest fundamentals of the poem: rhythm, rhyme, simple subjects — love, death, war."
— James Fenton, *The New Yorker*

"In the hands of an accomplished poet, a novel subject does as much as stylistic innovation to make a poem fresh and engaging."
—Dana Gioia, *Harvard Review*

"While it is true that we are initially *drawn* to poems by their passions, their questions, and their tonal urgencies, we are *convinced* by them, finally, insofar as they can invent formal means for their impelling motives."
— Helen Vendler, *The Breaking of Style*

"The pleasure we derive from a poem bears no relation to its subject. An elegy may provide more elation than an epithalamium. The darkest themes... provoke delight as well as sorrowful empathy when couched in well-wrought verse."
— Phoebe Pettingell, *Yale Review*

"The demise of poetry remains poetry's favourite subject. Like someone in a state of manic hypochondria, it continues to search for signs of its own ill-health."
— Simon Armitage, *PBS Bulletin*

On Anthologies:

"Anyone who makes an anthology is almost certifiably mad."
— Paul Muldoon, *Radio Ulster*

"Most anthologies are full of poems between three and six inches long."
— John Kerrigan, *The Irish Review*

"Reading anthologies is a bit like getting drunk on a series of miniatures."
— Robert Nye, *The Times*

"Anthology-making is a branch of poetry criticism, though in Ireland, increasingly, it seems to be the whole tree."
— Peter Sirr, *The Irish Times*

"Normally there is no class of book more slipshod, more boring, more prejudiced, more snobbish, more exclusive, more incestuous, more narrow-minded, more arid, more ignorant, more canonical, more soulless, more soul destroying, more anti-poetic than a poetry anthology. The shelves of bookshops are stacked with the spines of these prodigies of spinelessness..."
— Paul Durcan, *Lifelines 2*

"American critics are sometimes accused of being soft on Irish poetry, but the Irish are soft on it, too, as their proliferating anthologies indicate."
— Lucy McDiarmid, *New York Times*

"It is a sad truth — the anthologies and scholarly journals of the last fifteen years are evidence — that established Irish male poets, some with international reputations, were unhelpful and even obstructive in their attitude to the emergence of poetry by women."
— Eavan Boland, *Seneca Review*

"Every anthology published in my lifetime has been worthless as an account of contemporary literature... because of the form's spurious claim to completeness."
— Eiléan Ní Chuilleanáin, *Cyphers*

"Jealousy, rage, *amour propre*, factional in-fighting of Bosnian complexity — yes, another anthology of contemporary poetry has been published."
— Harvey Porlock, *The Sunday Times*

"The anthologies don't matter in the long run. They're like private clubs, sporting clubs where the editor is entitled to invite whom he/she wants to join. In time, genuinely 'androgynous' anthologies will be published, if the impulse for same is strong enough."
— Mary O'Donnell, *Graph*

"Mixed anthologies, like mixed social gatherings, have their advantages and their drawbacks. There's something to be said for excluding men, now and again, in order to give women a chance to come into their own."
— Wendy Cope, *Is That the New Moon?*

"Women's anthologies are read primarily by women. They could even be viewed as the up-market version of the woman's magazine."
— Carol Rumens, *Poetry Review*

"The institution of the anthology... is at best a convenience for teachers but otherwise a pernicious modern nuisance which keeps readers away from *books* of poetry."
— Thom Gunn, *Numbers*

"Usually the wider reading audience likes anthologies. They make life easier, and out of such books a reader can either widen or discover his or her own preferences; a little like window-shopping in poetry."
— Gerald Dawe, *The Irish Times*

On Themselves:

"I'm a stenographer of my mind. I write down what passes through it, not what goes on around me. I'm a poet."
— Allen Ginsberg, *The Irish Times*

"I'm an indoor nature poet."
— Eavan Boland, *Woman's Way*

"I wish somebody would parody me."
— Derek Mahon, *Rhinoceros*

"There's no posterity to write for. I'm writing now for mutated arthropods."
— Peter Reading, *Oxford Poetry*

"I think that the first significant influence on me was the beautiful heartbeat of my mother when I was resting inside her."
— Sharon Olds, *Slow Dancer*

"At the back of an extremely boring class one day, I was scribbling and suddenly the words came alive. It was an equivalent of one's first discovery of sex, a profound mental and psychic thrill. And I knew I was hooked."
— John Montague, *RTE 1*

"In my First Arts exam, I was given such poor marks in poetry that I had to switch to Archaeology and Medieval History. The poetry don informed me with a benign smile that I did not have a proper understanding of poetry."
— Paul Durcan, *Sunday Independent*

"I started a PhD in English at the University of Chicago because I loved poetry — which I now realise is like saying I studied vivisection because I loved dogs."
— Michael Donaghy, *Verse*

"As the aeroplane takes off, or the dentist drills into my tooth, I close my eyes and silently recite something by Shakespeare, Housman or Emily Dickinson. It doesn't banish fear but it helps prevent total panic."
— Wendy Cope, introducing *Poem for the Day*

"One of my favourite pastimes is listening to poetry on cassette in the car while driving. God help the poor sod who steals my car, and cranks up the stereo and gets Ezra Pound at full tilt..."
— Simon Armitage, *Verse*

"I wanted to be an artist, but everyone around me was saying I should be a criminal. I was a closet poet."
— Benjamin Zephaniah, *The Times*

"People like it when I write about dead queers; they just don't like it when I write about live ones."
—Thom Gunn, *Poetry Flash*

"It's the only way I can figure heaven to myself, that eventually one day you get into the poem and live there."
— Les Murray, *BBC Radio 3*

"Having to preach amongst rural folk, I've had to make myself intelligible. I've made my language simple because of that."
— R.S. Thomas, *Graph*

Poets on Poetry:

"A poem is like a radio that can broadcast continuously for thousands of years."
— Allen Ginsberg, *Channel 4*

"Poems are other people's snapshots in which we recognize ourselves."
— Charles Simic, *The Unemployed Fortune-Teller*

"Poetry subtly takes command of our breathing and dances with it; a sob built into a line will reverberate in the diaphragm and cause it to signal the brain for tears, and laughter can similarly be produced without any joke needing to appear in the text."
— Les Murray, *Meanjin*

"Fundamentally, what I want from poetry is the preciousness and foundedness of wise feeling become eternally posthumous in perfect cadence. Good poetry reminds you that writing is writing, it's not just expectoration or self-regard or a semaphore for self's sake. You want it to touch you at the melting point below the breastbone and the beginning of the solar plexus. You want something sweetening and at the same time something unexpected, something that has come through constraint into felicity."
— Seamus Heaney, *Salmagundi*

"A poem is a smuggling of something back from the otherworld, a prime bit of shoplifting where you get something out the door before the buzzer goes off."
— Nuala Ní Dhomhnaill, *RTE 1*

"A writer is not interested in explaining reality; he's interested in capturing it."
— Brendan Kennelly, *RTE Radio 1*

"Poetry requires a certain unworldliness."
— Blake Morrison, *The Daily Telegraph*

"Poets, real poets, whether they are flying toward it or away from it, are disbelievers in reality."
— Tony Hoagland, *Harvard Review*

"The pressure to record has always been the starting-point of poetry, now as 400 years ago, and if we disregard the primitive mnemonic urgency that underlies all writing, we do so at our cost."
— Thom Gunn, *Times Literary Supplement*

"Poetry resides in the unrepeatable perfection of its original articulation."
— Seamus Heaney, *The Sunday Tribune*

"Every poem is an answer to the question what poetry is for."
— Jamie McKendrick, *The South Bank Show*

"A poem can be an intense feeling, an intense description, a brief musical illumination of a philosophy — any of those and many other things."
— Thomas McCarthy, *Stet*

"Poetry's saving grace is that it is not a product. It is sister not to journalism or advertising, but to philosophy."
— Kathleen Jamie, *Poetry Review*

"Like philosophy, independent thought, and believing one's own nose, poetry perhaps has to be the province of the few."
— Herbert Lomas, *London Magazine*

"There is no reason to think that the odds against poetry that matters are any shorter in the twentieth century than they were in the eighteenth. Many are called but few, very few, are chosen; it is a lesson that we are happy to learn about everybody's lifetime except our own."
— Donald Davie, *Agenda Anthology*

"People wish to be poets more than they wish to write poetry, and that's a mistake. One should wish to celebrate more than one wishes to be celebrated."
— Lucille Clifton, *Poets & Writers*

"Poetry demands generosity of feelings; what else is it but an act of giving?"
— Jeremy Reed, *The Sunday Times*

"Poetry, because nobody agrees on what makes a good poem any more (if they ever did) excites rage, derision and misrepresentation... Secretly, everyone thinks she/he could do better."
— Philip Howard, *The Times*

"Virtue and poetry are not synonymous."
— Charles Simic, *Atlanta Review*

"A poem is a small, four-sided box, self-contained, which we construct or briefly inhabit to escape the world outside..."
— Ross Whitney, *Poets & Writers*

"If you make a good box, it's like making a good poem. You really have to get the corners squared if you're doing a quatrain."
— Derek Walcott, BBC Radio 4

"The best poetry opens a window in the reader's heart and mind. It's memorable, hummable."
— Maura Dooley, *Bloodaxe Books Catalogue*

"A poem is an attempt to find the music in the words describing an intuition."
— P.J. Kavanagh, *BBC Radio 3*

"For me, poetry is very much the time that it takes to unroll, the way music does...it's not a static, contemplatable thing like a painting or a piece of sculpture."
— John Ashbery, *Oxford Poetry*

"Sitting is for when you've got the poem going or you're revising it, trying to perfect it. But the original impulse needs to come out of movement."
— Fleur Adcock, *Acumen*

"Sooner or later even the poem I'm most proud of lies lifeless on the page before me, completely inert and without merit; and I have no idea where another will come from, or when."
— Anthony Hecht, *The Paris Review*

"It isn't good to dwell on something you have written and finished with — a poem when once abandoned should be left to make its own way in the world."
— Theo Dorgan, *The Furrow*

"A poem has to be the most powerful thing you can say in the shortest space possible."
— Charles Causley, *BBC Radio 4*

"Poetry is like solving a crossword puzzle in which you are also the compiler."
— Don Paterson, *The Observer*

"Finally, I don't believe in poetry as crossword puzzle, as being necessarily difficult."
— Paul Muldoon, *BBC Radio 3*

"Some poets are writing crosswords and more poets are writing algebra. I was never any good at crosswords and I'm hopeless at algebra. I'm not into the popular argument that poetry must be the lowest common denominator; let's have it the highest common multiple perhaps."
— Gabriel Fitzmaurice, *RTE Radio 1*

"Poetry is one of the few arts which is not menaced by not having an audience."
— Peter Porter, *BBC 2*

As the poet said

"I've heard my own work being denigrated as being mere pub-talk. If that's the case, I'm very happy with the comparison. Any poetry that confines itself to the merely literary is half dead. And I enjoy pubs a lot more than poetry readings".
— Ciaran Carson, *The Irish Review*

"The only people who have trouble with poetry are the people who link it with 'Literature'. It's much more akin to mountain walking and dancing by yourself at 2 a.m."
— Theo Dorgan, *The Irish Times*

"If I knew where poems came from, I'd go there."
— Michael Longley, *The Observer*

On Work:

"It is very important for a poet to organise a useful life. In our trade the life has to fit those moments when a poem becomes possible."
— Claude Vigee, *London Magazine*

"I keep Friday as... my poetry writing day, and I have to arrange for the Muse to attend between 10 am and 4 pm."
— Alison Chisholm, *Poetry News*

"It never does to let myself forget that, however hard it feels, writing poetry is usually a doddle compared with real work or real confrontation."
— Don Paterson, *Verse*

"That's the great thing about being a self-employed poet, you can give yourself lovely long holidays and EC grants and retire whenever you feel like it."
— Pat Ingoldsby, *The Northside People*

"I regard poetry... as a vocation. Any other work — freelance or bank-manager — simply supports the person writing it. There's no need for different hats."
— Carol Ann Duffy, *Verse*

"It may well be the unprofessional aspects of poetry — good poets come from all sorts of backgrounds and do every kind of job — that keep the art strong."
— Boyd Tonkin, *New Statesman & Society*

"Even a moderately interesting job outside the poetry workshop business is more likely to yield high poetic dividends than unlimited leisure or a work life confined to cajoling guileless youths into believing they are our next Rimbauds."
— Thomas M. Disch, *Parnassus*

"If you want to make a living as a poet, the last thing you'll be able to do is sit quietly and write poetry."
— John Morrish, *The Daily Telegraph*

"Poets are crippled by all demands imposed from the outside. The demands of the self and the demands of the language are what matter."
— Carol Rumens, *Fortnight*

"It does not take all day to be a poet and I have never understood the contentions of those eccentrics who think that a poet should not have to earn his living like the next man. Human nature is certainly not less noticeable in the ordinary world of work than it is to the genius who fancies solitude."
— C. H. Sisson, *PN Review*

"A full-time job kills a poet's talent — eventually. You can't treat the muse as a bit on the side with impunity."
— Fiona Pitt-Kethley, *Poetry Review*

"Having a full-time job and three children — perhaps those have driven my poetry out. It's very tough to retain the space which poetry needs."
— Blake Morrison, *Oxford Poetry*

"Women have often been told they must choose between children and artistic creativity. Helen Dunmore challenges the falsity of that choice, as her fifth collection of poems appears at the same time as her new baby."
— *Bloodaxe Books press release*

"I think the less a poet's job has to do with poetry the better... My work as a journalist doesn't get in the way of my poems. And it's the journalism which keeps bread on the table and keeps me in the street, where poems start."
— Seán Dunne, *RTE Radio 1*

"It is an immense discipline for a poet to work among people who think nothing of literature. And, after all, if poetry is about anything, it's about the same world that other people live in."
— C. H. Sisson, *Acumen*

"Being an artist is a disposition, a way of interpreting the world which is distinct precisely because it isn't and cannot be subsumed into a notion of career. Poets don't have careers, they have lives..."
— Ann Lauterbach, *American Poetry Review*

"I believe that it's the poet's job to redeem the ordinary world around us for the imagination and the spirit — even if that world is the suburb and office life."
— Dana Gioia, *Verse*

"Since most poets are teachers or academics, there are certain areas of life that poetry rarely touches. When was the last time you read an office poem or a factory poem that wasn't dull or patronising?"
— Adam Thorpe, *The Observer*

"I work very long hours, until two or three in the morning and often with a lot of tension and stress. I find that reading a few poems is the escapism I need."
— Colin O'Daly, chef, *The Sunday Press*

"Parents still prefer their children to be taxidermists and tax collectors rather than poets."
— Charles Simic, *Michigan Quarterly Review*

On Love & Marriage:

"A shy postman didn't stand a chance with the island's most beautiful woman until the great poet of love gave him the courage to follow his dreams and the words to win her heart."
— Advertisement for *Il Postino*

"If you're a man and you want to really please a woman, do you necessarily write a poem? I'm not convinced... There are other things I should do — and maybe cleaning the kitchen floor is one of them."
— Ian Duhig, *BBC 2*

"The test of a desirable poem is not that one wants to marry it immediately but that one wants to meet it again — soon."
— Kevan Johnson, *Poetry Review*

"The poem that says 'I love you' is the little black cocktail dress, the classic thing that everyone would like to have written one of."
— James Fenton, *BBC Radio 4*

"We've become a pessimistic society. We don't want poems of love."
— Miranda Seymour, *BBC 2*

"Poets now... are afraid of writing love poems unless they are also somehow seen to be political."
— Peter Sirr, *RTE Radio 1*

"The best love poems confirm something we secretly felt but never said."
— Tess Gallagher, *The Observer*

"Every new poem is like finding a new bride. Words are so erotic, they never tire of their coupling."
— Stanley Kunitz, *The Language of Life*

"A successful happy marriage poem, like a happy marriage itself, is a triumph over the unlikely. You must write it with the inventive care with which you would write science fiction."
— Stephen Dunn, *Seneca Review*

"I think it's natural for poets to become friends, but I also think, after a certain time, it's very difficult for poets to keep a friendship alive — for example, I've always felt that if two poets marry, the marriage has to be almost impossible."
— Yehuda Amichai, *The Paris Review*

"You can't have two poets living together — it doesn't work. There's only a certain amount of creative energy available in the household."
— Fleur Adcock, *RTE Radio 1*

"Our relationship is remarkable because it's allowed our writing to flourish."
— Penelope Shuttle, on her marriage to Peter Redgrove, *Independent on Sunday*

"When I said I wanted to marry a poet, I saw it as living in this marvellous harmonious meeting-of-two-minds way, but I didn't think about having children or doing the ironing or any of that sort of stuff."
— Elspeth Barker, *Independent on Sunday*

"If your dirty-weekend date came to bed with a Laura Ashley nightie and a thin volume of Emily Dickinson, you too might turn nasty."
— Allison Pearson, *Independent on Sunday*

"I lied in my ad. I hate Wallace Stevens."
— Caption to cartoon of a dating couple, *The New Yorker*

"I think all poetry is erotic. It's the Pleasure Principle. You could spend the afternoon in bed with your mistress or writing the poem and it would use the same sort of energy."
— Medbh McGuckian, *The Irish Review*

On Sex:

"Sex, drugs and rock 'n' roll are taking a backseat to poetry among the hip set."
— Headline, *Time*

"There is no poetry without sex, not even in Alexander Pope..."
— Anthony Burgess, *The Sunday Times*

"What appears erotic to a male writer doesn't necessarily appear so to a female."
— Roz Cowman, *Graph*

"Poems are pleasure first: bodily pleasure, a deliciousness of the senses."
— Donald Hall, *Op. Cit.*

"I think all poetry is erotic. It's the Pleasure Principle. You could spend the afternoon in bed with your mistress or writing the poem and it would use the same sort of energy."
— Medbh McGuckian, *The Irish Review*

"Most of my poetry is post-coital. People should make love a great deal and direct the feelings they get into creative work."
— Peter Redgrove, *Staple*

"The trouble with much modern poetry is that it's nothing but sex chopped up on the page."
— Quoted anonymously in *Acumen*

"A thousand naked fornicating couples with their moans and con-tortions are nothing compared to a good metaphor."
— Charles Simic, *The Gettysburg Review*

"More than ever before the erotic is available to women as theme or metaphor."
— Linda France, *Sixty Women Poets*

"Metaphor sleeps around."
— Alfred Corn, *Salmagundi*

"When I reduce everything, being a poet is the rhythm that's inside my body which is identified as sexual."
— Sharon Doubiago, *Poetry Flash*

"The promiscuity suggested is such that one wonders whether the ISBN isn't, in fact, his telephone number."
— Carol Ann Duffy, reviewing Alan Jenkins's poetry, *The Guardian*

"In all literate societies, the idea of poetry has been inextricable from the idea of love. It is almost as if that particular kind of patterned utterance is a mating call of some kind."
— Germaine Greer, *Channel 4*

"I'd have loved to give him mouth-to-mouth recitation."
— Caller to Gay Byrne Show, in a reference to Omar Sharif, *RTE Radio1*

"In the old days, critics used to call sex scenes 'poetic' in the hope of warding off the district attorney. (Unlike porn, poetry is not expected to be exciting...)."
— Stuart Klawans, *Parnassus*

"Of course girls fall for poets — it's false modesty to say they don't."
— Hugo Williams, *The Observer*

On Money:

"Poets and money are seen in each other's company only rarely."
— Michael Ellison, *The Guardian*

"There's no money in poetry. On the other hand, there is no poetry in money."
— Philip Howard, *The Times*

"Poets, uniquely among creative artists, can't hope to make a living from their art."
— John Ashbery, *BBC Radio 4*

"I think it's insulting to poets and writers to single them out and say: 'We can't give you wages'. We can give wages to absolutely useless people like advertising executives and to the VAT man (who is an absolutely destructive influence on society) but you'll be much more revolutionary if we don't give you any money."
— Adrian Mitchell, *BBC Radio 3*

"Of almost £3,000,000 distributed last year, authors of Plays and Poetry scored 0.18% — or about £5,500."
— John Sumsion, on Public Lending Rights, *Stand*

"In many ways, poetry is the art form of the recession. A poet's overheads are negligible."
— Rick Jones, *The Guardian*

"Without language there is no poetry, without poetry there's just talk. Talk is cheap and proves nothing. Poetry is dear and difficult to come by."
— Charles Wright, *Quarter Notes*

"There is no price that can match the value of the words of the poet."
— Michael D. Higgins, State Reception for Seamus Heaney

"Murray was born with the poet's equivalent of a silver spoon in his mouth — as a farmer's son."
— Adam Thorpe, on Les Murray, *The Observer*

"In our culture, money is elitist, not poetry."
— Jeff Hansen, *Poetics*

"Poets and writers are given wads of money about as often as Hale–Bopp makes an appearance."
— Michael McDermott, *The Sunday Independent*

On Drink:

"A wallop of a fist which would give you a black eye is a relatively harmless piece of machinery in comparison to a cut from a drunken poet who, with two lines, will leave you a mark for the rest of your life that will go on even into future generations."
— John B. Keane, *Radio Ulster*

"I often think my life would be much richer if... I'd gone to pubs all the time."
— Stephen Spender, *The Financial Times*

"Nobody could drink the way I did and not be more than half in love with the poetic benefits of cracking up in different ways."
— Brendan Kennelly, *Dark Fathers Into Light*

"Poets, and Irish poets, perhaps, in particular, are not noted for sobriety..."
— Philip Hensher, *The Spectator*

"In a poet, too much sobriety is a dangerous thing."
— Tony Hoagland, *Harvard Review*

"Poetry is relaxation from the labours of inebriation."
— Quoted anonymously in *Acumen*

"He was once told by doctors that if he took another drink he would be dead. His response was to call in at the nearest bar on the way home."
— Peter Waymark, on Charles Bukowski, *The Times*

Poetry Wars:

"To the outsider poetry is a peripheral activity, useful if you're in love or on the Underground; to poets and their satellites it is a battleground, bristling with factions and militant tendencies."
— Daisy Goodwin, *The Guardian*

"Apparently no literary discipline gives rise to as much heated controversy and embittered mud-slinging when placed under any form of critical scrutiny as does contemporary Irish poetry. Often we are gripped by what can be most charitably described as 'poetry wars'..."
— Fred Johnston, *The Irish Times*

"Poets by their nature fight perpetually against one another, even as the original bards thundered against one another in the causes of their respective warring chieftains."
— Owen Dudley Edwards, *New Welsh Review*

"How many attempts to get poetry on the road have foundered because the poetry entrepreneurs have rolled all over the tarmac trying to gouge out each other's eyes?"
— P. J. Kavanagh, *The Daily Telegraph*

"I, Adrian Mitchell, do challenge you, Professor James Fenton, to a Public Poetry Bout..."
— Adrian Mitchell, *New Statesman & Society*

"Heavyweight boxing is a tame, almost gentle, spectacle compared with the contests of literary men."
— Richard Boston, *The Guardian*

"There are *jealousies* rolling about like loose cannon in the Groves of Poesie — not much chinking of money, but plenty of *grinding of teeth*."
— John Whitworth, *The Spectator*

"The sense of ferrets fighting for mastery of a septic tank is depressing — poetry is the national art, after all..."
— Sean O'Brien, *The Guardian*

"No-one in a literate culture is able to kill their enemy with a poem, though no doubt a good many would like to try."
— Martin Duwell, *Scripsi*

"It is safe to assert that the culture of poetry — i.e. backbiting — is ubiquitous. If I were Noam Chomsky I might even say that it is part of the deep structure of the brain."
— Peter Forbes, *Poetry Review*

"American poetry — a world as fractious and as riven as any Trotskyist cell."
— Stephen Schiff, *The New Yorker*

Presidents & Princes:

"Poetry is the true flavour of the new regime."
— Gerald Barry, on the Robinson Presidency, *The Sunday Tribune*

"I like the company of poets. They take you away from the boring realities of life, if you like, and open up all sorts of new exciting things, sometimes quite startling."
— Charles J. Haughey, *The Irish Times*

"Mr Haughey resorted to poetry yesterday to attack his former partners in coalition..."
— News Report, *The Irish Times*

"Not many of our politicians are poets, though all of our poets are politicians."
— Stan Gebler Davies, *The Independent*

"All his life he dabbled in poetry."
— Olivier Todd, on François Mitterrand, *The Sunday Times*

"I've spent years studying form — and I'm not talking about racing!"
— Michael D. Higgins, *Hot Press*

"Practically every person I've met in the European Commission tells me they're a poet."
— Mary Banotti, *The Sunday Press*

"Happy people on the whole don't write poetry."
— Denis Healey, *BBC Radio 4*

"Poetry is conservative: poets are members of the establishment, college professors, the intimates of Presidents, members of cabinets, cornerstones of official study groups."
— Frank Flanagan, *Children's Books In Ireland*

"On the matter of poets, I have one question and it is this —
where are the soaks of yesteryear?"
— Liz McManus, *The Sunday Tribune*

"Politicians deal with issues; poets deal with epiphanies."
— John Agard, *BBC 2*

"I would like to advise those who think that in the President's
chair sits a poet, dreamer and naive fellow, that even a poet has
teeth."
— Vaclav Havel, *The Sunday Tribune*

"There is an element of almost complete freedom and frankness
that can be experienced in a poem — not always the case in the
political world."
— Jimmy Carter, *Interview*

"He has 203 volumes of poetry — compared with 373 on horses
and 352 on ships."
— Anthony Holden, on Prince Philip, *The Sunday Times*

"How many statespersons are remembered for what the poet said
of them rather than what they achieved!"
— Michael D. Higgins, State Reception for Seamus Heaney

"As the court jester had unique licence to mock the monarch in his
or her presence, so does the poet use his or her gifts to improve or
in some way change the established order."
— Malcolm Williamson, *The Times*

"People in the West don't know me. Their image of me is distort-
ed. They don't know that I am a poet, for example."
— President Gaddafi of Libya, *Newsweek*

On Politics:

"Politics is a local, transient business in which a week is a long time, whereas poetry, or at least the better sort, is universal and enduring."
— Terry Eagleton, *The Irish Times*

"What kind of a politics is poetry advocating if it is not populist? How can poetry effect political change without an audience to hear it?"
— Lucia Perillo, *Michigan Quarterly Review*

"It seems to me that poetry should deal with something more important than politics."
— Irina Ratushinskaya, *BBC 1*

"As far as politics is concerned, the poet's most important work is to fiddle while Rome burns."
— Robert Crawford, *Times Literary Supplement*

"A poet is a politician against his will."
— Yevgeny Yevtushenko, *The Irish Times*

"I'm not a political writer and I don't see literature as a way of solving political problems."
— Seamus Heaney, *The Irish Times*

"Language is not neutral. It's very much a political tool. It's charged with prejudices. So a poet who says 'I'm not in politics' is not being realistic."
— Chinua Achebe, *The Sunday Tribune*

"I am a poetician, not a politician."
— Yevgeny Yevtushenko, *The Financial Times*

"Now we are able to use all the words in the vocabulary."
— Daniela Crâsnaru, Romanian poet, *BBC Radio 4*

"Violent movements which contain poets are more dangerous than ones which don't."
— Conor Cruise O'Brien, *RTE 1*

"The revolutionary poem in Ulster now tends to be an elegy. It resists any notions of selective mourning."
— Michael Longley, *BBC Radio 3*

"There is no use coming to poets, either in Soviet Russia or Northern Ireland, and expecting or ordering them to deliver a certain product to fit a certain agenda, for although they must feel answerable to the world they inhabit, poets, if they are to do their proper work, must also feel free."
— Seamus Heaney, *The Irish Times*

"There's no point in writing poems on political subjects simply to go on the record on the right side. Poetry had better be interesting always, it had better be fresh always, and so the sort of poem that simply says 'don't drop the bomb' is of no interest to me."
— Richard Wilbur, *American Poetry Review*

"A bad poem is bad enough, but a bad poem about something as big as The Troubles is an impertinence and an offence."
— Michael Longley, *BBC Radio 3*

"It's all too typical for contemporary poets to write as if they assume that the social importance of what they advocate — justice for women, the environment, the poor, etc. — gives importance to the self-identity of the poet, as if suffering can be 'borrowed'."
— Judith Kitchen, *The Georgia Review*

"There seems to be an assumption that the artist in any form has a responsibility to address topical issues. It's so dreary. It's why Northern poetry has become so dehydrated. They've a sense of the eyes of the world watching them."
— Aidan Carl Mathews, *The Sunday Tribune*

"War and poetry have come to seem to belong together, like love and songs, or landscape and painting."
— Jeremy Treglown, *Independent on Sunday*

"War poetry is the one literary genre that one hopes will never be extended."
— Bernard Bergonzi, *PN Review*

Words or Muse–ic:

"Prose is for the sun and the day — poetry is for the moon and the stars and night."
— George Mackay Brown, *Poetry Wales*

"Prose is walking; poetry is flying."
— Galway Kinnell, *KQED Radio*

"What makes poetry reach beyond prose is its joyful recognition that there is more to words than meaning alone."
— F.R. Jones, *Comparative Criticism*

"Fourteen lines of a sonnet can bring you to the point of feeling that takes a novelist 70,000 words."
— Stanley Cook, *Cambridge Contemporary Poets 2*

"Poetry isn't just shorter than prose. It isn't just a matter of lines that don't go to the edge of the page. It's about having some extra life in it; having more packed into less."
— Alan Jenkins, *Writers' Monthly*

"A poet's job is to write poetry and you are rather going to exhaust the Muse if you write too much prose... It is a betrayal for a poet to adopt prose."
— R.S. Thomas, *BBC Radio 4*

"Most books offered as poetry never leave the condition of prose — which is not to say they are good prose."
— Edna Longley, *London Review of Books*

"One of the differences between prose and poetry is that in poetry there is no second order... There's no beginner's luck, no first, second and third league. There's only one league and we wish to be in that one league of poetry which inheres in the language and stays."
— Seamus Heaney, *RTE Radio 1*

"Prose may be the more difficult art, but poetry is the higher, the only discipline that can really save language from corruption and misuse. Poets are indeed the unacknowledged legislators of mankind, since poetry offers the only language that can in the end reshape the world."
— Peter Ackroyd, *The Times*

"Most poetry is shorter and goes further than prose because it can dispense with 'that's the reason why', and 'And I suppose I ought to say'."
— Peter Forbes, *The Guardian*

"Surely there is nothing — *nothing* — that poetry can do that prose cannot do, *except* to the extent that its effect has to do with measure."
— Stephen Yenser, *The Southern Review*

"With a lyric poem, you look, and meditate, and put the rock back. With fiction you poke things with a stick to see what will happen."
— Margaret Atwood, *New York Times*

"It's not what the world is that poetry is primarily concerned with, but what the world feels like. The novel relates; the poem tries to leave unsaid as much as possible."
— Charles Simic, *Harvard Review*

"Poetry gets landscape and weather for its subjects; the novel gets boxing and tattooed women and sex."
— Craig Raine, *The Independent*

"Misprints! One simply cannot have such a thing in a book of verse between covers: quite a different standard is applicable from that appropriate to prose."
— Hilary Corke, *The Spectator*

"The difference between a book of poems and a novel is around £5,000."
— Dermot Bolger, *The Irish Times*

"The main difference nowadays between poetry and prose is that, dreadful though it is, poetry doesn't go on for nearly so long."
— 'Bookworm', *Private Eye*

Novelists on Poetry:

"A poem almost exists because of the pattern of space around it."
— Fay Weldon, *BBC 2*

"I often think of my novels as sonnet sequences."
— John Banville, *RTE 1*

"The dud poet may fool us for a while, but not the dud novelist."
— Gabriel Josipovici, *Times Literary Supplement*

"Poets have one great advantage over novelists that is seldom noted, their artistic longevity."
— Thomas M. Disch, *Parnassus*

"Poetry contains almost all you need to know about life."
— Josephine Hart, *The Observer*

"Most poems get ruined by having too many ideas in them."
— Michael Ondaatje, *Writers' Monthly*

"Poetry is a different area of the brain (from fiction) — much closer to music and mathematics."
— Margaret Atwood, *BBC Radio 3*

"We read poetry on the printed page as fast as we like — faster than we should — whereas we listen to music in its own time."
— J.M. Coetzee, *New York Review of Books*

"Why has the experimentalism of the avant-garde, which has failed in the novel, succeeded in poetry? Because poetry is *always* experimental; while the novel, on the contrary, by its nature, cannot be... Which is to say that experimentalism is synonymous with poetry and that, applied to the novel, it leads simply to the substitution of the novel with poetry."
— Alberto Moravia, *The Threepenny Review*

"The best poets inhabit the world with quicker senses than most of us. In town or country, they see, smell and hear more."
— Margaret Drabble, *The Forward Book of Poetry*

"I wish I could open a magazine now with the same excitement with which I once opened *Nimbus* to find a Kavanagh poem."
— John McGahern, *New York Times*

"Fiction requires willpower; poetry requires the abdication of willpower."
— Margaret Atwood, *BBC Radio 3*

"You can never leave poetry behind."
— Dermot Bolger, *The Irish Times*

Who Reads Poetry?

"Poetry has removed itself by its own choice into something that is private, that comes out in little magazines, that only other poets read."
— Derek Walcott, *Outposts*

"Poetry is read only by poets and that's its sickness."
— Carol Rumens, *Poetry Review*

"The most generous interpretation of the putdown 'Only poets read poetry' is that poems *make* us into poets."
— James Richardson, *Poetry*

"You have this myriad of books that are being published which no one reads, which in a sense are being published more for the writer than for the reader."
— Dana Gioia, *BBC Radio 3*

"People don't read poetry because poetry is not as widely available as trash, or as thrillers. I think if I were a publisher, a publisher concerned for poetry (which is a rare bird to find!), I would publish anthologies that would be sold in supermarkets. You never know what people buy in supermarkets!"
— Joseph Brodsky, *Vogue*

"There has always been a lot of interest in reading poetry. But it has tended, particularly in bookshops, that poetry sections should be put in the back. A bit like pornography, poetry is always to be found in the dark recesses."
— Desmond Clarke, *BBC Radio 4*

"A poetry bestseller is any book that sells four or five copies in any given store."
— Michael Wiegers, *Hungry Mind Review*

"People read poetry to bathe their forehead in the well of reality. To refresh themselves."
— Paul Durcan, *The Sunday Independent*

"It is the job of the poet to make the reader cry."
— Michael S. Harper, *The Language of Life*

"Unless we read poetry, we'll never have our hearts broken by language, which is an indispensable preliminary to a civilised life."
— Anatole Broyard, *New York Times*

"She is knee deep at the moment in the poems of Lez Murray, Paul Dacre and Ivan Boland." (*sic*)
— Amanda Armstrong, on Carol Ann Duffy, *Writers' Monthly*

"You are writing in the dark if you read no one but yourself. And in the dark you can't even read yourself properly."
— Peter Sansom, *Writing Poems*

"There's far too much written. People should take a sabbatical from writing and do more reading."
— Mark Strand, *American Poetry Review*

"I realize, increasingly, that I sit down to a new book of poems much in the same way I take my place in the dentist's chair: I may benefit from the experience but it won't be a pleasure."
— Stephen Dobyns, *New York Times*

"No one writes without being aware that readers come to any new text, as it were, with pistol cocked and an interrogator's scowl: 'Does this bard have anything to say that I have to listen to, or can I just terminate proceedings right now?' "
— Alfred Corn, *Poetry*

Reviewing:

"Criticism is our jailer. Poetry should be sprung from it so that it is as natural a form of reading as a novel."
— Les Murray, *The Independent*

"Some people seem to be more cruel about poetry than about fiction or other books; and there are certain reviewers who, if you've had any sort of success, it's anathema to them."
— Elizabeth Jennings, *BBC Radio 4*

"Having cold water thrown over your dreams is part of being a writer."
— David Wheatley, *The Irish Times*

"I think most critics would agree that poets are 'the irritable race'. Given a mixed review, a poet usually fastens with a vengeance on a critic's one misgiving."
— Alice Fulton, *Parnassus*

"Humiliation is the invariable lot of poets, but each poet, and each new generation of poets, learns to be humiliated in different ways."
— Blake Morrison, *The Guardian*

"...the little world of poetry has thousands of inhabitants, each of them convinced that someone who dislikes or reprehends their work must be motivated by a personal vendetta or a deep-rooted enmity towards what is true and beautiful."
— Thomas M. Disch, *The Castle of Indolence*

"Poetry, more than most writing forms, is an incestuous business, and competent reviewers are likely to be, if not inimical to the reviewee, or married to/living with/slavishly devoted to/pupil of him or her, then in some way bound symbiotically to the author under scrutiny."
— Richard Pine, *Irish Literary Supplement*

"You can't review a book if you're not prepared to be rude about it if you don't like it."
— Wendy Cope, *The Dark Horse*

"Criticism often anaesthetizes the lion with which the poet struggled."
— Roger Little, *PN Review*

"Good poetry speaks for itself. The only worthwhile commentary on it is that which falls short of the power and meaning of the text. At best this falling short tells us of the vital circle which a poem draws around itself to guard its obstinate radiance, to refuse paraphrase or critical domestication. Only weak poetry is explicable; only over weak poems can criticism achieve its jealous mastery."
— George Steiner, *The Sunday Times*

"A description of a poem is as much fun as a description of a joke."
— Don Paterson, *PBS Bulletin*

"Conditions for reviewing are far from ideal: good poems require rereading and rereading; they need to be lived with before we know them. Meanwhile, editors have their deadlines. Publishers and booksellers lose interest if reviews don't appear within a year of publication. And the flood of books continues."
— Alfred Corn, *Poetry*

"Extensive praise given to weak books, especially when the books are written by potentially fine poets, is harmful both to the art as a whole and to the poets' evaluation of their own work; it tends to perpetuate the poetry's weaknesses."
— Dick Allen, *The Hudson Review*

"Reading reviews of modern poetry is like attending prize-giving in a small, caring primary school: everyone has done terribly well, it's all absolutely marvellous."
— Harvey Porlock, *The Sunday Times*

"An honest, descriptive, detailed, clarifying criticism keeps poetry healthy — it's poetry's weedkiller and, to the extent it encourages what's best in writing, it can nourish poetry too. No good growth without good gardeners."
— Douglas Dunn, *Acumen*

"The horrible truth is that very few people in today's literary world have the capacity to make an independent judgement about poetry. They pay lip-service to the great poets of the past whose stature was established by discrimination of the kind they lack, and today they rely, if they bother at all, on publicists' hype."
— Peter Forbes, *Poetry Review*

"Criticism is misdirected creativity."
— Nuala Ní Dhomhnaill, *RTE Radio 1*

On Life:

"Poetry, perhaps more than any other literary form, expresses the desire and need to be at home in the universe; to belong."
— G.J. Finch, *Critical Survey*

"Poetry will not teach us how to live well, but it will incite in us the wish to."
— David Constantine, *Poetry Review*

"Poetry says more about the psychic life of an age than any other art. Poetry is a place where all the fundamental questions are asked about the human condition."
— Charles Simic, *American Poetry Review*

"A poem is simply an adaptation of experience."
— Bernard O'Donoghue, *The Irish Times*

"Many poets struggle to make connections between the lumpy thing called Real Life and the shiny thing called Poetry."
— Ian McMillan, *Poetry Review*

"People do seem to need poetry; it makes life feel less bleak by giving you something encouraging for a change."
— Elaine Feinstein, *The Times*

"It is in battling with life and tasks that one becomes a fit person to speak in poetry. I think a poet must in some way engage with the world. I don't think an ivory tower is a good place to write poetry."
— Kathleen Raine, *BBC Radio 3*

"Ours is probably the only language in the world that permits the word 'poet' to be thrown as a jocular insult."
— Andrew Billen, *The Observer*

As the poet said

"Every hospital should have a poet. Every prison, every school. Every building. Every store. There are enough of us. It can all be done."
— Sharon Olds, *Poets & Writers*

"It seems to me that there are a million poets that write interesting verse, but I can't think of a single one that I would think of getting up in the morning and going to to find my life profoundly changed and enlightened and deepened by."
— A.R. Ammons, *Michigan Quarterly Review*

"If we look at this century, an extremely small part of human experience has been fixed in language and literature. We may wonder how small a percentage of what mankind has lived remains in the language."
— Czeslaw Milosz, *Partisan Review*

"In poetry there is a nostalgia for something we have forgotten and which poetry, nevertheless, remembers."
— Juan Malpartida, *Agenda*

On Death:

"This is one sense of poetry. A little concoction of words against death. It's almost the instinct against death crystallized."
— Miroslav Holub, *Times Literary Supplement*

"Sometimes I think the last sound in the world will be Yevtushenko beating on his drum. There is something apocalyptic about his self-promotion."
— Michael Hofmann, *The Times*

"I doubt that many people now want to read verse that is realistic about death. They are more likely to be moved by verse which in effect denies that death happens at all."
— John Casey, *The Daily Telegraph*

"As soon as you are not moving in poetry, you are dead. Mere repetition is like the onset of freezing."
— David Constantine, *PBS Bulletin*

"Poets are like pigs, only worth money when they're dead."
— Ted Hughes, *The Independent*

"Nobody these days knows a poet is alive until he or she is dead."
— Philip Howard, *The Times*

"Donal Russell's last wish was to have his body skinned and his hide tanned like leather for face-binding volumes of his poetry."
— News Report, *The Irish Press*

"There is something wonderfully amenable about dead poets. The live ones are riddled with egotism and acidity, a skinless sensitivity to slights and an immoderate estimation of their own talent, not to mention an insatiable need for money and appreciation."
— Andro Linklater, *The Sunday Times*

"Great poetry is seldom 'positive', in the way the media today is always telling us everything from politics to poetry ought to be. Great poetry is more often one of the voices of death."
— John Bayley, *Agenda*

"There's nothing to write about death, unless you believe in an afterlife."
— Thom Gunn, *Agni*

"After poets are food for worms, they are food for biographers."
— William Logan, *Parnassus*

"He very nearly killed me on his bicycle one night... What a way to die — under a bike cycled by a poet in the dark!"
— John Ryan, recalling Monk Gibbon, *RTE Radio 1*

On Prayer & Spirituality:

"Poetry has to do with the non-rational parts of man. For a poet, a human being is a mystery... this is a religious feeling."
— Octavio Paz, *The Independent*

"Poetry is essentially the soul's search for its release in language."
— Joseph Brodsky, introducing *Apollo in the Snow*

"I think the ultimate function of the poet is to praise. It may have taken somebody like Dante the long pilgrimage through the *Inferno* and the *Purgatorio* to get up to the praising point but nevertheless that is the end vision."
— John Montague, *Irish University Review*

"I feel that all poetry is prayer, it's just as simple as that."
— Jean Valentine, *American Poetry Review*

"The kinds of truth that art gives us many, many times are small truths. They don't have the resonance of an encyclical from the Pope stating an eternal truth, but they partake of the quality of eternity. There is a sort of timeless delight in them."
— Seamus Heaney, *The Economist*

"A poem is a kind of rhythm between the world and the spirit or soul."
— Daniel Berrigan, *Agni*

"Poetry is the voice of spirit and imagination and all that is potential, as well as of the healing benevolence that used to be the privilege of the gods."
— Ted Hughes, *Times Literary Supplement*

"Poetry can tell us what human beings are. It can tell us why we stumble and fall and how, miraculously, we can stand up."
— Maya Angelou, *The Independent*

"If poetry can't cope with what God means in the late 20th century, then it doesn't deserve to remain a major art form."
— R.S. Thomas, *The Independent*

"I think to be reading your poetry as a breadwinning activity... commits some sin against the freedom of poetry. I do believe that poetry is in the realm of the gift and in the realm of the sacred."
— Seamus Heaney, *Christian Science Monitor*

"The first and last lines always come to me on a direct line from God. I just have to fill in the middle."
— Kate Clanchy, *Harpers & Queen*

"The cardinal sin of a poet is to be dull."
— R.S. Thomas, *Independent on Sunday*

Poetry Makes Nothing Happen:

"Auden's conviction that poetry makes nothing happen was inexact. Bad poetry makes nothing happen, largely because bad poets make nothing happen to poetry — they cannot excite the form, so the form can hardly be expected to excite the world."
— James Wood, *The Sunday Correspondent*

"Poetry is not about making things happen. That's what language does. Poetry is about making language happen."
— Donald Revell, *American Poetry Review*

"According to the most advanced theories, poetry can say nothing that is not ultimately about language. But if a poet writes believing that all his or her discoveries are ultimately about poetry itself, that poet will produce bad or minor art."
— Robert Schultz, *The Hudson Review*

"Contrary to what Auden may have thought at one time, I do believe that poetry makes things happen: learning to say words in a different way may lead us to look at the world in a similarly different fashion."
— Jordi Doce, *Agenda*

"As well as between tongue and teeth, poetry happens between the ears and behind the left nipple."
— Douglas Dunn, *The Observer*

"You cannot earn your living at poetry; it makes nothing happen; the audience is tiny and as often as not composed of fellow-aspirants seeing whether you are up to something they should take into account; you are reviewed among a clutch of your fellows at a length even a crime novelist might resent. The reward is that elusive, extraordinary rightness no other art achieves, the aesthetic equivalent of the hole-in-one."
— Grey Gowrie, *The Daily Telegraph*

As the poet said

"Nothing happens in poetry. A poem is just a moment."
— Sara Berkeley, *Sunday Independent*

"Who says that writing doesn't have any effect? I had a bucket of excrement dumped on my head for daring to criticise the North-east..."
— Sean O'Brien, *The Independent*

The Unconvinced:

"No one is ever better for writing good poetry; but, more importantly, no one is ever better for reading it."
— Editorial, *The Times*

"Anybody who describes his vocation as poet, purveying the modern style of formless verse, is invariably among the meanest and most despicable in the land: vain, empty, conceited, dishonest, dirty, often flea-ridden and infected by venereal disease, greedy, parasitical, drunken, untruthful, arrogant... all these repulsive qualities, and also irresistibly attractive to the women."
— Auberon Waugh, *Literary Review*

"Poets are not like the rest of us. To start with, they are untidy, often failing to tuck their shirts into their trousers; they are shockingly unpunctual, and much given to talking to themselves. Some, even more reprehensible than the rest, drink more than is good for them, and others beat their wives (assuming they married them in the first place, which is by no means certain)."
— Bernard Levin, *The Times*

"It has long been a demonstrable fact that the poet as personality is a cranky, off-putting, pain in the butt. Bumptious, bilious, and babbling; irresponsible, irreal, and well irrigated; lewd, loud-mouthed, and lunatic, he does not present an edifying spectacle to the society that he must portray for the delectation of succeeding generations."
— Fred Chappell, *The Formalist*

"Having breakfast with poets is often like breakfasting at the zoo — with the added excitement of not knowing whether you're going to eat with the friendly chimpanzees or grizzly bears with sore heads!"
— Patricia Oxley, *Acumen*

"I have noticed on arts programmes that poets and so forth are often described purringly as possessing a 'childlike' vision or dealing with the big wide world in a 'childlike' way. Presumably this means that they are always knocking things over, tearing things up and screaming blue murder if they don't get their own way."
— Craig Brown, *The Sunday Times*

"A poet is allowed to walk into a pub with a bandaged thumb and explain that he did it banging in a fence-post, to fall off a horse with no whit of social opprobrium ensuing, to cast a fly-rod and remove his neighbour's earlobe with no more consequence than an indulgent smile from his hooked victim, to empty his 12–bore at a standing pheasant, miss it by yards, and shatter the village church's one decent medieval window without anyone shouting anything more critical than 'Oh, bad luck!' "
— Alan Coren, *The Times*

"One is encouraged to think that poets are lonely, dysfunctional people; that they phrase things in a way that cannot be understood, possibly because they don't know what they are trying to say; that they are miserable sods; that they are pretentious; that they are tweedy and old-fashioned, or else impossibly, annoyingly glamorous."
— William Leith, *Tatler*

Notes for Younger Poets:

"It takes years and years to gain any mastery over the old traditional forms. And I think every poet should go through that apprenticeship."
— George Mackay Brown, *BBC Radio 4*

"Most poets who offer advice to a poet should be ignored, because they want you to be just like them, only not quite so good."
— Adrian Mitchell, *Poetry Review*

"It is not so difficult to kindle the poetic fire in the first place as to keep it going, hot and bright, through a whole lifetime."
— Thom Gunn, *Agni*

"I think for a poet the struggle from the beginning is to really find the confidence and authority of your own voice, not only in terms of historical style but how to get to the point where what you're writing on the page is, metrically and in terms of the tone, the exact voice in which you speak."
— Derek Walcott, *Radio Ulster*

"In youth, poems come to you out of the blue. They're delivered at your doorstep like the morning news. But at this age, one has to dig."
— Stanley Kunitz, *New York Times*

"We assume that poets, like chess champions or mathematical prodigies, burn themselves out."
— Adam Mars-Jones, *BBC Radio 3*

"I suspect that a famous adolescent anxiety is never very far from a poet's mind... It is: 'Am I doing it right?' "
— Jeffrey Wainwright, *The Poet's Voice and Craft*

"Poets grow in different ways, some in skill, others in range."
— Robert B. Shaw, *Poetry*

"Poets have a responsibility to write serious reviews and essays about their contemporaries, even when the prospect seems daunting. Call it literary jury service."
— Joel Brouwer, *Harvard Review*

"The working conditions for young women poets are infinitely poorer than the conviviality and congratulations that surround their male counterparts."
— Eavan Boland, *Irish Literary Supplement*

"Younger poets, impatient to win recognition, find the realm of poetry has a limited number of laurels for the large number of would-be recipients."
— Katie Donovan, *The Irish Times*

"One danger I see for young poets is that recognition can come too soon. There are too many people on the watch for young Irish poets, and too many people ready to pounce as soon as a poet has published half a dozen poems."
— Harry Clifton, *Metre*

"I wish I had a pound (or ten) for every time I have read the words 'one of Ireland's most exciting young writers': it's inflationary, and it's not fair on the writers because they might start to believe it."
— Rodney Pybus, *Stand*

"I felt that my first poems were trying to write like stained glass but that I would like to write a poetry of window glass."
— Seamus Heaney, *BBC Radio 3*

"Poets, seeing their inner life solidified and exposed on white pages, may well wish to change it in the light of later experience. But while we gain with age, we also lose. There are poems written at twenty-five which are beyond the writer of fifty."
— Helen Dunmore, *Poetry Review*

"There is an apprenticeship to poetry as there is to most decent things. But nowadays this apprenticeship is passed over in favour of the ready-made, the immediate."
— Fred Johnston, *Books Ireland*

"The greatest difficulty for the poet is how to go on being one."
— Michael Hofmann, *London Review of Books*

"Poets, because they should never completely grow up, must continually come of age."
— Michael Longley, *Irish University Review*

"It seems to me that ageing is a subject that, by and large, women poets deal with better than men, in that they are more likely to rise above being merely grumpy and depressing."
— Wendy Cope, *BBC Radio 4*

On Readings & Workshops:

"Poets used to flake out in foreign parts from an excess of emotion and TB. Not any more — now the complaint might be poetry circuit fatigue. Too many readings, TV appearances, book signings. For poetry is Fashionable."
— Jane Speed, *Elle*

"If half the poets out there reading their old poems would stay home and write some new ones, our literature would be vastly enriched."
— Robert Phillips, *New York Times*

"When you meet the usual haunted-looking individuals who organise readings — men with eyes red from crying, women with garlands in their hair — they have either just taken over from someone who committed suicide, or are trying to pass the job on to someone whose sanity is still intact."
— Hugo Williams, *Times Literary Supplement*

"Poetry reading is an art form, like drama is an art form."
— Nuala Ní Dhomhnaill, *Studies*

"The reading of poetry in public is a largely perfunctory act. You learn the mannerisms, the gimmicks, the over-emphasis of certain words — just like actors do."
— R. S. Thomas, *The Independent*

"It would be very odd to go to a concert hall and discover that the pianist on offer *wasn't any good at all,* in the sense that he couldn't actually play the piano. But in poetry this is an experience we have learned to take in our stride."
— James Fenton, *Ronald Duncan Lecture*

"Some poets make bad performers because they are more concerned with presenting themselves than their poems."
— Michael Glover, *The Independent*

"Certain readings can still look and feel like the last meeting of the most eccentric followers of some obscure, dwindling and discredited religious movement."
— Simon Armitage, *Poetry Review*

"My great happiness about poetry readings is that they're a mechanism for widening the circle — ten times as many people will come to a reading as will buy a book. You're reading over the heads of the elite..."
— Les Murray, *PN Review*

"Most people's idea of poetry readings as being a boring, stifling affair is fairly accurate."
— Pat Boran, *The Irish Times*

"Although the current club poetry scene is perhaps better linked with stand-up comedy, or folk music, it has invigorated 'page poetry'. Few of us who read our work in public can afford to be meek or stuffy."
— Anne Rouse, *PBS Bulletin*

"There are writers of verse — now, more than ever — who, before an audience, chant or drone or strut or mince or yammer or harangue, but very few can read their work so as to keep their listeners constantly aware of the beauty of sense, however complex, and the sense of beauty arising from the powerful, delicate, and compelling ways in which that sense is made by poetry."
— John Hollander, *Poetry*

"That's one reason I never go to poetry readings — poems are always over before I've cottoned on to them."
— Charles Causley, *The Financial Times*

"I've always found most poetry readings comparable to jazz... Both involve a small group of people making a lot of noise, and then, just when you think it's all over, it carries on."
— Jaci Stephen, *Daily Mirror*

As the poet said

"Babies are not brought by storks, and poets are not produced by workshops."
— James Fenton, *Ronald Duncan Lecture*

"Poetry doesn't really lend itself to guides, manuals and confessions, any more than sex does. It says eat me and drink me. Alice didn't need any further instructions, and nor should we."
— William Scammell, *Independent on Sunday*

"The workshops, which have a monopoly on the training of poets, encourage indolence, incompetence, smugness and — most perniciously — that sense of victimization and special entitlement that poets have now come to share with other artists who depend on government or institutional patronage to sustain their art, pay their salaries, and provide free vacations."
— Thomas M. Disch, *The Hudson Review*

"The effect (of writers' workshops) on editors is, of course, to increase their workload. It means that we have yet more quite polished, but fundamentally mediocre material to plough through."
— Joy Hendry, *Acumen*

"A lot of poetry is a kind of soliloquy — and therefore one has no audience!"
— Sorley MacLean, *BBC Radio 4*

Language, Rhyme & Reason:

"It may be, though I can't prove it, that certain bromidic ideas about form are losing their power over us. The idea, for example, that metre and stanza are intrinsically repressive and right-wing, whereas free verse is liberating and democratic. The idea that free verse is forever original and venturesome, that it is somehow 'experimental' to imitate Pound or Bill Williams decade after decade."
— Richard Wilbur, *PN Review*

"The thing about poetry, especially poetry in metre and rhyme, is that it draws attention to its own physicality. It is air made physical."
— Tony Harrison, *BBC Radio 3*

"Good metrical rhymed verse, if it's to grip the imagination and stay readable, has to have, as well as those external formal features, the same dynamo of hidden musical dramatic laws as the apparently free verse."
— Ted Hughes, *The Paris Review*

"Metrical poetry is ultimately allied to song, and I like the connection. Free verse is ultimately allied to conversation, and I like that connection too. Not many poets can mix the two."
— Thom Gunn, *The Paris Review*

"You get bad poems that rhyme and bad poems that do not. Rhyme is not what sorts them out, and neither is it an infallible way of producing good writing."
— Michael Hofmann, *The Times*

"Free verse has become a banal reflex. A lot of poets imagine that it reflects the fragmentation of the social world or something. In fact, it is just sloppy writing."
— Justin Quinn, *Independent on Sunday*

"It is the struggle to express the contemporary that makes poetry seem alive, and contemporary life can hardly be expressed in the forms used by poets four hundred years ago."
— Louis Simpson, *Harvard Review*

"You can't write a poem until you have a form. It's like... trying to play an untuned instrument."
— Les Murray, *The Independent*

"Form cannot be first if you want to reach high artistic levels, since you are then bound by form, and that form is very often a betrayal of reality. It cannot grasp reality."
— Czeslaw Milosz, *Partisan Review*

"At times, I've suspected that too heavy an emphasis on the technical side of poetry reduces it to the level of car maintenance or flower arranging."
— Douglas Dunn, *PBS Bulletin*

"I'm inclined to agree with my friend U.A. Fanthorpe that it's a bit like wearing a corset."
— Elizabeth Bartlett, on rhyming, *Poetry Review*

"A poem without lines, without metre of some kind is the literary equivalent of a vegeburger."
— John Greening, on prose poetry, *Poetry Review*

"If every generation wrote with the voice it knew from the past, contemporary poetry would still be in the style of Chaucer or Shakespeare."
— Alison Chisholm, *Writers' News*

"There is a shortfall between what language can express and what an individual can feel; metaphor can go some way towards bridging that gap."
— Simon Armitage, *BBC Radio 4*

"Compared to ordinary language, poetry can be like ice-skating compared to walking."
— Robert Pinsky, *New York Times*

"The poem has to be an organism — a self-sustaining ball of life. Not just a splurge of words, which happens to be nearest the heart or off the top of the head."
— Christopher Reid, *The Sunday Times*

"The problem with most free verse is that it locates wisdom in the self and not in the language."
— Glyn Maxwell, *Bloodaxe Books Catalogue*

"There ought to be a store of the best language somewhere, and poetry is one of the last few fortresses in which it could be kept and guarded."
—Alan Brownjohn, *Acumen*

"We didn't have metaphors in our day. We didn't beat about the bush."
— Fred Trueman, *BBC Radio 3*

As the poet said

"Translation is like describing one animal in terms of another. What you read outside its original language is a convincing rhinoceros, but the actual poem is an elephant."
— Fergus Chadwick, *Acumen*

On Translation:

"Of the tight-rope acts of language, that of the translation of poetry is the most defiant. There is no safety net."
— George Steiner, *The Sunday Times*

"Translation is like describing one animal in terms of another. What you read outside its original language is a convincing rhinoceros, but the actual poem is an elephant."
— Fergus Chadwick, *Acumen*

"The notion that *some* verse translation is automatically better than none cannot be contested often enough."
— Clive Wilmer, *The Times*

"Like a wet gobstopper rolling across a carpet, a poem crossing into a different language tends to pick up fluff."
— Francis Spufford, *The Guardian*

"Okay, so perfection in the sense of 100% equivalence is unattainable — but why should translators of poetry, of all people, be blamed for not attaining what the carpet-weavers of Islam know to be the attribute of God alone?"
— Francis Jones, *Poetry Review*

"Translating someone's work, poetry in particular, has something about it akin to being possessed, haunted. Translating a poem means not only reading it deeply and deciphering it but clambering about backstage among the props and the scaffolding."
— Alastair Reid, *The New Yorker*

"'Prosaic' might describe the pleasure of translated poems, like lovemaking overheard from behind a closed door, where the listener hears the sound evoked by each caress but does not feel it on her skin."
— Suzanne Gardinier, *Parnassus*

"Living with poetry in translation is like living with strangers: what often begins in beautifully romantic exoticism concludes in misunderstanding, impatience and, sometimes, hostility."
— Sam Hamill, *American Poetry Review*

"I believe in bad translations, because... they awaken the reader's intuition. Whereas a good translation confines the material to its own achievement."
— Joseph Brodsky, *Verse*

"It is one of the bitter truths of life that all poetry, whether great or less great, is untranslatable. Whereas music is universal, each good poem is ultimately shut off inside its particular language, and there is no way of appreciating its unique effect apart from knowing that language, and knowing it well."
— John Weightman, *Independent on Sunday*

"Translating a poem into another language is rather like setting it to music."
— Edward Lowbury, *Acumen*

"Every translation is a performance of the text."
— Piotr Kuhiwczak, *The Observer*

"Where most translations fail is by choosing what is possible in English, rather than what is right in English."
— Craig Raine, *Thumbscrew*

"Nothing — not words, not phrases, not even metres — mean precisely the same in one language as they do in another."
— George Szirtes, *New Life*

"Even very famous poets when they're going through a rough patch in their own creativity resort to translation. It is almost like they're assimilating other people's work into their own particular voice."
— Louis de Paor, *Irish Studies Review*

"I don't feel good about two or more translations of a single poem. It's like the man who always knew the exact time when he had just one watch, but from the moment he had two watches he never knew what time it was."
— Miroslav Holub, *Poets & Writers*

"To be a good translator is somewhat like being a good double-agent."
— Julia Older, *Poets & Writers*

"In Estonian, the lovely word for 'poet' — *luuletaja* — also means 'liar'."
— Sally Laird, *The Observer*

Seamus:

"Bellaghy Celebrates as Farmer's Son Wins Top Literary Award."
— Headline on Heaney's Nobel Prize, *Farmers Journal*

"Patience, politeness, attentiveness to his interlocutors, a thoughtful hesitancy, a smiling but never smarmy Irish charm — in a world where most writers are raging paranoids or egomaniacs, such qualities go a long way."
— *The Observer*, in a profile of Seamus Heaney

"Heaney... is very shrewd, able and level-headed, a natural diplomatist — something rare among poets, who are often silly and hysterical people, seeing enemies under every bed or desk while feverishly indulging in inept intrigues of their own."
— Brian Fallon, *The Irish Times*

"Nobel is one of the few magic words in the world. It blesses the art of poetry."
— Seamus Heaney, *The Times*

Light Verse:

"Good light verse is harder to write well than more serious poetry; so much depends on technique and careful craftsmanship."
— Elizabeth Jennings, *Daily Telegraph*

"Trying to print light verse in this country nowadays is like trying to peddle mink coats at a convention of militant ecologists."
— X.J. Kennedy, *Parnassus*

"The poem is primarily a piece of music, but in the twentieth century, it must be music for our own age... Conventional metres and conventional rhyme schemes, as far as I am concerned, can nowadays only be used for light and occasional verse."
— John Heath-Stubbs, *Poetry Book Society Bulletin*

"In the worlds of alcohol and yoghurt, the word 'Light' (or Lite) is used to indicate that the product is good for you but not much fun. In the world of poetry, the word 'Light' (or Comic) is used to suggest that the product is fun but not much good for you."
— Mark Lawson, *The Independent*

"Whether it's a question of can't or won't, few poets are funny on the page. Poets who do entertain are in danger of being considered lightweight, as if humor and seriousness were mutually exclusive."
— Alice Fulton, *Poetry*

"It is a mistake to say that because a poem gets a laugh or elicits a sigh that it succeeds *as a poem*."
— Fred Johnston, *Books Ireland*

"*Instant Poetry*: Everyone's a poet with this ingenious kit... Open the box to find 425 words and word fragments — more than enough to compose a pithy haiku, a provocative love poem, a saucy limerick, or a sonnet to rival Shakespeare."
— Advertisement, *The New Yorker*

As the poet said

"All poems about cats are essentially cute and lightweight, even those about trying to murder them."
— Don Paterson, *Times Literary Supplement*

"Nobody writes poems about parsnips."
— Anna Pavord, *The Independent*

"He certainly knows his onions, and his parsnips."
— Valentine Cunningham, on Craig Raine, *European English Messenger*

Heavy Verse:

"... people are afraid to read 20th century poetry. It is too compacted, too intense, too uncompromising. It never allows you to relax into it. It seems to be a cerebral pact between the poet and a small, devoted audience of initiates; and the understanding and, God forbid, the enjoyment of poetry can only be the consequence of strenuous intellectual effort."
— Michael Glover, *The Financial Times*

"Some modern poetry has become so 'difficult' that it is incomprehensible to many intelligent, well-read people who are quite capable of understanding sophisticated works of fiction, philosophy and science."
— Peter Reading, *The Sunday Times*

"To the familiar complaint that poetry is too difficult and elitist and should adapt itself to its potential audience, it must be replied that when poetry makes overtures to populism it ceases to be itself."
— Sean O'Brien, *The Printer's Devil*

"The charge frequently levelled against poetry nowadays of being difficult, obscure, hermetic, and whatnot indicates not the state of poetry but, frankly, the rung of the evolutionary ladder on which society got stuck."
— Joseph Brodsky, *Poetry Review*

"It is no denigration of a poem to say that it resists its audience for a while."
— Seamus Heaney, *RTE Radio 1*

"I don't mind a poem being difficult if the writer is saying a difficult thing, but if they're only difficult to give an impression of profundity — 'Pooh', says I."
— Norman MacCaig, *PN Review*

"Too many poems are all meaning and no reserve."
— Medbh McGuckian, *Irish Literary Supplement*

"I think we are beginning to lay too much emphasis on accessibility in the wrong way. Of course, it should be accessible, but it might be accessible through the feelings it arouses rather than through the actual act of mental comprehension."
— Anthony Cronin, *RTE Radio 1*

"The most difficult thing to do in a poem is to present ideas."
— Robert Pinsky, *TriQuarterly*

"A poem becomes alive at just that point when it escapes what it was 'meant' to be."
— Bruce Murphy, *Poetry*

"A poem cannot be seen to strain after profundity; it must arrive like an astonished, unerring sleepwalker."
— K.E. Duffin, *Harvard Review*

"Many weak poems substitute vagueness for mystery."
— Stephen Dobyns, *Best Words, Best Order*

"The folly of the rage for meaning is to treat a poem like a locked box to be broken into for its contents, then thrown away."
— Theodore Weiss, *American Poetry Review*

"Writing poetry is difficult. It is a peculiar, lonely, onanistic activity."
— Ciaran Carson, *The Daily Telegraph*

"Let poetry be difficult, very difficult, the difficulty of a deep ocean, but not obscure, the obscurity of a muddy shallow little lake."
— Peter Viereck, *Parnassus*

"The most difficult thing in the world is to be clear."
— Paul Muldoon, *Independent on Sunday*

"The most difficult thing is the generation of excitement. That is why poets are so panic-stricken. They are afraid that the unexpected, accidental kickstart that sends poems into action will desert them."
— Seamus Heaney, *The Sunday Times*

"It is a very scary thing to be shown a poem for the first time."
— Marie Heaney, *The Irish Times*

Journalists on Poetry:

"Poems are the SAS of the army of words, they are an elite. Poetry is the muse by which all other art is measured."
— AA Gill, *The Sunday Times*

"The elites have been writing and composing for themselves for too long. The poems that people like do conform to the traditional criteria; they rhyme, they have rhythm, they have internal resonance."
— Kevin Myers, *Times Educational Supplement*

"Poetry is not in the business of taking Polaroids: it should be a long slow developer, raising images that we frame and keep."
— Allison Pearson, *Independent on Sunday*

"Poetry's very shape puts us in a receptive mood; the words are framed in music."
— Con Houlihan, *Evening Press*

"One of the things that good poetry does is that it keeps the eye open while everyone else is flinching."
— Clive James, *BBC Radio 4*

"I've always believed that men who recite poetry, who are the most magnificently attentive, are also the most callous."
— Chrissy Iley, *The Sunday Times*

"Poets are the *Big Issue* sellers of the literary world. Some are silent and desperate, others mad and messianic. You know you ought to buy their wares, but suspect you won't enjoy them..."
— Suzi Feay, *Time Out*

"I don't mind poetry so long as I don't have to read it."
— Lynn Barber, *The Daily Telegraph*

Critics (and Poet-Critics) on Poetry:

"Poetry remains our most concise, affecting and memorable way of speaking. It allows us to say the things that move us most deeply and stay most fixed in our minds. It is also one of our few ways of holistic experience."
— Dana Gioia, *The Irish Review*

"In the hands of any real poet, poetry exists at the very heart of the language. It is always 'difficult' because, by its very nature, it is saying things that verge on the unsayable."
— Bryan Appleyard, *The Sunday Times*

"When one remembers how many separate talents go to make a formidable poet — talents musical, imaginative, psychological, visual, intellectual, metaphysical, temperamental — one wonders that the thing is done at all."
— Helen Vendler, *The New York Review of Books*

"Many critics consider themselves superior to the work of literature, especially when the work expresses a personal or subjective experience. They know so much more than the poem, and they forget that the poem is what they know."
— Denis Donoghue, *Times Literary Supplement*

"What a poem should do is present something in order to convey the feeling. It should be precise about the something and reticent about the feeling."
— Doris Corti, *Writers' News*

"Poetry can be reticent without being obscure."
— Dana Gioia, *Poems of Love*

"To be a poet of the obvious, one has to write supremely well."
— Peter Denman, *Irish University Review*

"...the things that distinguish good poetry from bad — an invincible rhythm, a mastery of construction, a thesaurus of cultural imagery, arresting linguistic vitality."
— Helen Vendler, *New York Times*

"It is not necessarily that 'more means worse', but that arguments about better and worse seem beside the point when everyone gets into print."
— Edna Longley, *The Southern Review*

"You may well think that no great poetry is being written today. I could not possibly comment, except to observe that great poets come as single spies, not in battalions... And the single spies come in unexpected disguises, and are not immediately recognised."
— Philip Howard, *The Times*

"What's so striking at the moment is we seem to have got away from the Great Man syndrome. It is poetry which is flourishing rather than a few privileged individuals."
— Anthony Roche, *RTE Radio 1*

"There is something to be said against merely good poetry: It steals attention away from the best, and, indefatigable as crabgrass, chokes out the more endangered species."
— Alfred Corn, *Poetry*

"Usually, I think there's nothing to be said about mediocre poetry. It's like being a talent scout for an opera company, when all you can say about the voice you hear is, 'No, it has no carrying power, it hasn't any capacity to stay on pitch, it hasn't any sense of innate rhythm, it hasn't any expressive color, it hasn't interpretive power... it's just no, no, no.'"
— Helen Vendler, *The Paris Review*

"The thing that is wrong with the poetry world is that in it the poets and the critics are the same people."
— Anna Adams, *Acumen*

On Madness & Neurosis:

"To be a published poet is not a sane person's aspiration."
— Bernard O'Donoghue, *Oxford Poetry*

"In the twentieth century, I think, in the English-speaking culture, a poet is somebody who is in some way effeminate or strange, incomprehensible, and not quite right."
— Eiléan Ní Chuilleanáin, *The Canadian Journal of Irish Studies*

"Writing a poem is a bit like being sick. It is quick and efficient and you always feel better afterwards."
— Sarah-Jane Lovett, *The Sunday Times*

"For the serious poet, art is anything but therapeutic. Sylvia Plath's poetry did not alleviate her tragic illness... Dylan Thomas's fluid out-pourings of words did not cure his alcoholism."
— Leah Fritz, *Acumen*

"A survey of leading 18th century British and Irish poets... found a strikingly high rate of mood disorders, suicide and institutionalisation.'"
— Ben MacIntyre, *The Times*

"Poets were... five times more likely to be depressed than scientists, and fifteen times more prone to it than soldiers."
— Rebecca Fowler, *The Sunday Times*

"Next time you feel a bit under the weather, give the pills and potions a miss and try reading — or writing — some poetry. That is the advice of doctors who are taking part in a Bristol University study which shows that sometimes a few lines of Wordsworth, Keats or Browning can overcome a patient's need for minor tranquillisers."
— Paul Stokes, *The Daily Telegraph*

"A lot of the writing that's going on at present, far from being therapeutic, is an essay towards a collective nervous breakdown."
— Ciaran O'Driscoll, *Cyphers*

"Twenty-seven poets had nervous breakdowns, fifteen committed suicide, and fifteen were/are diagnosed as alcoholic. Nineteen served time in jail, fourteen died in battle, three were murdered, one executed. Zany professions include lumberjack, tax inspector, furniture remover, carpet salesman and policeman..."
— Ian Hamilton, on the poets in his *Oxford Companion to Twentieth-Century Poetry*

"Writing helps me stay out of psychiatric hospitals."
— Pat Ingoldsby, *The Big Issue*

"I think I am too normal to be a 'real' poet."
— Miroslav Holub, *Poetry Review*

"The one thing that can get a poet irritated and upset is the thought of another poet's poems."
— Charles Baxter, *Michigan Quarterly Review*

On the Land of Saints and (God help us) Scholars:

"Ireland is where you can't throw a stone over your head without hitting a poet."
— Thomas Kilroy, *Times Literary Supplement*

"Poets are old and most of them should be shot. Irish poetry is staid, boring and controlled by the 35 pluses who are mostly academics and are looking backwards instead of forwards."
— Olaf Tyaransen, *Connacht Tribune*

"Ireland is one of the very few countries where you can be reactionary stylistically and still be considered absolutely relevant."
— Peter Porter, *Metre*

"Like everything else in Ireland, poetry is contentious. There is always an occasion of outrage."
— Denis Donoghue, *New York Review of Books*

"If you leave aside the handful of Irish poets that everyone has heard of, it's tempting to lump together the remainder as unmemorable. There they sit, all writing away, as though poetry had become a matter of lessons learned, influences assimilated and risks eschewed."
— Patricia Craig, *Times Literary Supplement*

"Irish poets today, whatever their local or religious affiliations, speak in more collective tones than other poets writing in English. They are Irish almost before they are poets."
— John Bayley, *New York Review of Books*

"With so much negative discussion of poetry in the United States... it has been a tonic to live in a country where poetry enjoys a vital, secure place in the national culture."
— Richard Tillinghast, *AWP Chronicle*

"Dublin is a very powerful and intense and abrasive atmosphere for poets, and anyone who has lived there knows that it is as far as a poet can get from a flattering environment!"
— Eavan Boland, *Poets & Writers*

"In Ireland, even today, you can still walk about Dublin and hear people talking a sort of English which would strike an Englishman immediately as being very poetic. The whole language hasn't become ironed out by commercialism and relationships with the rest of the world."
— Stephen Spender, *Irish Literary Supplement*

"How does one explain the recent flowering of poetry in Ireland, with a population one-fiftieth of ours and a literature easily the equivalent of our own? Is it the relative absence of television addiction in Ireland? The centrality of literature to the national culture? The open sore of the Northern Ireland conflict as a stimulus to national self-definition?"
— Richard Tillinghast, *New York Times*

"The Irish poetry scene is very much a hothouse kind of thing and there's terrible pressure on you to publish a book every three years or every five years and keep your reputation alive."
— Michael O'Loughlin, *RTE Radio 1*

"Since the mid-1970s, Ireland has seen a remarkable surge in the writing and publishing of poetry with the result that the market-place is very active. With few exceptions, however, the media indiscriminately see all this activity as 'a good thing' and rarely bother to examine the situation sensitively and judiciously."
— Gerald Dawe, *Irish Literary Supplement*

"No doubt because the universities and the pubs of Ireland appear to be so heavily populated by them, it's symptomatic of the national complacency to see the poet rather than to know the work."
— Eileen Battersby, *The Sunday Tribune*

Women on Women — with the odd man thrown in:

"A woman is so naturally fluid and her mind is so dominated by her body, that for a woman to write real poetry — as men traditionally have been able to do - is difficult."
— Medbh McGuckian, *Irish Literary Supplement*

"When the history of poetry in our time is written — I have no doubt about this — women poets will be seen to have re-written not just the poem, not just the image... They will have altered the cartography of the poem. The map will look different."
— Eavan Boland, *Irish University Review*

"Must it be said that, for all the trumpeting about women poets, the empress has no clothes? That she is a Lady Godiva after all?"
— Derek Mahon, *The Irish Times*

"All male poets are amazingly opinionated; I have never met one who wasn't."
— Wendy Cope, *The Times*

"Some poets would do well to bear in mind the fact that we are all either male or female and that it's egregious to make too much of one or the other."
— Patricia Craig, *Poetry Review*

"I was (and still am) in no way conscious that a woman poet's task, with respect to skill, differs in any way from a man's."
— Anne Stevenson, *Poetry Wales*

"It is still a political act to publish a book of poetry by women."
— Jo Shapcott, *Bloodaxe Books Catalogue*

"Is (sartorial) imagery peculiar to women's writing? Men don't write poems about trousers."
— Peter Denman, *Cobweb*

"It is not reasonable in a poet to expect the applause of society. She is a troublemaker by profession, one who looks under carpets, one who notices that the emperor is wearing designer clothes. She must be independent to the point of eccentricity and is often, though not necessarily, as curst as a crow-trodden hen and as odd as one of the triple-faced holy monsters with which the Celts depicted Ogma the omniscient, gazing in all directions at once."
— Biddy Jenkinson, *Irish University Review*

"Irish women poets were publishing at a substantial rate during the nineteenth century. Contemporary women poets may be writing out of silence, but it is the silence of ignorance, brought about through the time's neglect of their maternal literary heritage."
— Anne Colman, *The Irish Review*

"Marjorie Perloff remarks to me that fewer and fewer men are taking literature courses, and she is afraid the whole discipline will become 'feminized', as in trivialized, marginalized. Poetry as women's work, like needlepoint."
— Ann Lauterbach, *American Poetry Review*

"Feminism remains a superb tool of analysis for discovering why a woman did not write a poem. It is of no value whatsoever in judging the poem that she wrote."
— Eavan Boland, *Verse*

"At its deepest level — you may say at the level of ontological underpinning — the Irish poetic tradition is sexist and masculinist to the core."
— Nuala Ní Dhomhnaill, *RTE Radio 1*

Interviewer: "Does it make any difference to you being a woman poet?"
Liz Lochhead: "I don't know. I've never tried being a man poet!"
— *BBC Radio 4*

"Words like 'best' are competitive, male words, unfitting to any discussion of poetry, especially women's poetry. What we want is not hierarchy but infinite variety."
— Gillian Clarke, *Bloodaxe Books Catalogue*

"No woman has ever written an epic poem nor ever will. They have certain minor gifts. The great gift of woman is being a woman."
— Kathleen Raine, *Acumen*

"Woman's creativity does not demand the right to build monuments that will loom in the minds of people yet unborn. Women's art is traditionally biodegradable, and women's poetry may be no exception."
— Germaine Greer, *Times Literary Supplement*

Joann Gardner: "I know in Ireland, women writers don't know where to go for their examples."
Grace Paley: "Well, they should go to life, forget the fucking literary people..."
— *American Poetry Review*

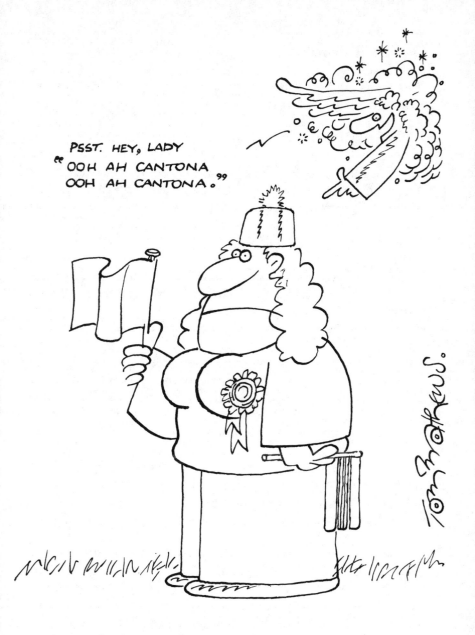

"What are football fans' chants, except the vernacular folk–poetry of our time?"
— Richard Morrison, *The Times*

On English Poetry:

"One wonders how it is that English poets ever manage to make great poetry out of a language that can sound as emotionally shy as ours."
— Michael Glover, *Financial Times*

"In this country, poetry is just lyrical spun sugar — a sweet irrelevance; but in countries which have suffered repression and the control of language... poetry matters and is about important themes."
— James Wood, *The Guardian*

"With British poets there so often seem to be only two or three reasonable poems in any one volume. There are very few books worth *buying*, which is very saddening."
— Dannie Abse, *The New Welsh Review*

"We hear a lot from socially self-conscious poets and very right-on, PC poets, who talk about bringing poetry to the people as if it was some sacred mission, like converting the natives to Christianity. But most of us don't give a toss."
— Michael Donaghy, *The Independent*

"National Poetry Day has a flavour of charitable enterprise, a flag day for the culturally disabled, with celebrities rattling a tin at you in the gaps between the programmes."
— Thomas Sutcliffe, *The Independent*

"Englishmen first started blushing in the proximity of verse between 1890 and 1910. We must blame the pre-Raphaelites, Swinburne, Rossetti and Co. At this time we developed our national image of the poet as a vague, hypersensitive, unpunctual, sexually ambiguous drip who is always in love, drunk, drugged to the eyeballs and perpetually unable to cope with the world."
— Stephen Pile, *The Sunday Times*

As the poet said

"Perhaps the key factor that has been missing for English poets since the war has been the audience; the kind of audience that has other things to do than to read poetry, and therefore comes to it with a direct expectation of usefulness."
— Felicity Rosslyn, *PN Review*

"When one looks at the progress of post-war English poetry it is like watching a dinosaur take side-steps in wet concrete."
— Jeremy Reed, *Lipstick, Sex and Poetry*

"Developments in Britain since the Sixties show that poets and people do not have to be oppressed for their mutual appreciation to be heightened."
— Editorial, *The Independent*

"What are football fans' chants, except the vernacular folk-poetry of our time?"
— Richard Morrison, *The Times*

"My argument with English poetry of the post-Philip Larkin era is the denigration of it to a sideline: when you're not being a civil servant, you write poetry at the weekends. I think poetry demands more than that; it demands a total sacrifice."
— Jeremy Reed, *RTE Radio 1*

"We have eaten, we have lived, we have breathed Keats for three days. It's like eating steak and ice cream for three days."
— Ione Kemp Knight, after a Keats conference, *New York Times*

"Keats was the first poet I got really excited about. In fact, I was rather in love with him until I found out how tall he was."
— Wendy Cope, *The Daily Telegraph*

"It happens to be a poem that I heartily loathe, with its smarmy Cockney view of beauty..."
— John Montague, on Keats's 'Ode to a Nightingale', *New York Times*

"'Christ in heaven', a young man exploded to me some years ago, 'Twas a great pity Keats didn't shoot that fuckin' nightingale!'"
— Brendan Kennelly, *Journey into Joy*

"It is the legend of the life of John Keats we must blame for the fact that poetry is not an acceptable topic of conversation among grown men in public houses."
— Michael Glover, *The Independent*

"In our time no greater misfortune can befall an English poet than to be made Poet Laureate."
— Stephen Spender, *The Independent*

"The average face, the average voice, the average life — that is, the life most of us lead, apart from film stars and dictators — had never been defined so precisely in English poetry until Philip Larkin."
— Derek Walcott, *New York Review of Books*

"So much in the life, and quite a bit in the work, exudes a repellent, smelly, inadequate masculinity."
— Bryan Appleyard, on Larkin, *The Independent*

"Philip Larkin: The Minor Talent of a Foul-Mouthed Bigot"
— Front page announcement, *The Times*

"A death-obsessed, emotionally-retarded misanthropist who had the impudence to generalise his own fears and failings to the way things are."
— Terry Eagleton, on Larkin, *Channel 4*

"For me personally, it is very important to give a spiritual dimension to poetry. I am definitely against such poets as Philip Larkin."
— Czeslaw Milosz, *Partisan Review*

On American Poetry:

"There is very little real poetry coming out of America at the moment because they have tried to harness Pegasus to the university and have turned it into a carthorse just plodding along."
— Les Murray, *BBC Radio 3*

"There are probably at this moment in this country more than a hundred lyric poets writing between the ages of 22 and 67 who are all capable of greatness and who have all written individual poems that are astonishing in their beauty and originality. So, I think, it's very possible that what we're experiencing is a Golden Age of American Poetry."
— Norman Dubie, *American Poetry Review*

"No one can say that America has been inhospitable to the Irish poets. On the contrary, we apparently prefer them to our own domestic product, greeting them with praise and university employment as soon as they present themselves."
— Alfred Corn, *Poetry*

"Being honoured by your country is a wonderful thing. Especially in a country where poets are for the most part a harmless impertinence like birds at an airport."
— Howard Nemerov, on accepting the National Medal of the Arts in the U.S.A.

"Look at rap — that's the best poetry being written in America at the moment; at least it rhymes."
— Derek Mahon, *The Sunday Times*

"A multiple choice 'Hipness Test' contest held at a Manhattan shopping mall included the question, 'The latest trend in club entertainment is...?' The correct answer: poetry reading."
— Marcia Biederman, *Poets & Writers*

"From what I've gleaned from American poets, survival is tough, self-assertion essential, the morbidly sensitive are submerged."
— Medbh McGuckian, *The Irish Review*

"Sylvia Plath's 'Daddy' set a standard for modern unfairness, and gave birth to a genre of American poetry in which the author insults her nearest and dearest."
— James Fenton, *Independent on Sunday*

"American poetry is full of 'Oh, poor me.'"
— Mark Strand, *The New Yorker*

"More and more of us, it seems, want to disclose the worst about ourselves and our intimates. A mode of discourse initiated by Robert Lowell's *Life Studies* and Anne Sexton's *To Bedlam and Part Way Back* has trickled down to Oprah Winfrey and *People* magazine."
— Michael Vincent Miller, *New York Times*

"William Carlos Williams was responsible for encouraging more dud poets than anybody in this century except Ezra Pound."
— Julian Symons, *The Sunday Times*

"He virtually invented 'flower power' and the fashion for bald, bearded men in home-stitched sandals."
— Obituary of Allen Ginsberg, *The Times*

Genius & Originality:

"One of the nasty aspects, that has become a kind of orthodoxy about poetry, is the view that in any one generation only two or three poets can be of any value. That's rubbish. It was always rubbish."
— John Lucas, *BBC Radio 3*

"Allegedly we are surrounded by geniuses. Everybody is becoming more proficient. *Everybody* is a poet. People use with ease big words like Art and Culture. It's *frightening*."
— Lawrence Durrell, *The Sunday Times*

"'Inimitable' is one of those off-the-shelf, unhelpful epithets that get loosely tossed in the direction of mastery, but in poetry the test of true originality is to be eminently imitable — it's doing it first and registering the trademark that counts."
— Peter Forbes, *The Independent*

"Time, familiarity and imitation are the implacable enemies of artistic originality. Who now is jolted by the surprise in Haydn's 'Surprise' symphony?... Perhaps nowhere in English literature have time, familiarity and imitation played greater havoc with original work than with Wordsworth's."
— Norman Fruman, *Times Literary Supplement*

"One is always surprised by the drumstroke in Haydn's 'Surprise' symphony, no matter how many times one has heard it, and one is always interested by a poem that genuinely contains a mystery."
— T. J. G. Harris, *PN Review*

"To the embarrassment of many scribblers, this biography confirms that poetry requires some mysterious agency of the unconscious — call it inspiration."
— Edna Longley, on Jon Stallworthy's *Louis MacNeice*, *The Irish Times*

"The characteristic dilemma facing the poet is this: psychologically he needs recognition and approval, and yet he knows he cannot hope to achieve it unless he is to aim at being the elegant media-man who confines his productions to what oft was thought but ne'er so well expressed. Alienation is thus the necessary consequence of originality, and originality is the only prize worth striving for."
— Adam Czerniawski, *Poetry Review*

"To put it crassly, in order to make his work sell, as well as to avoid cliché, our poet continually has to get to where nobody has ever been before — mentally, psychologically or lexically."
— Joseph Brodsky, *Times Literary Supplement*

"Poets today... are afraid of revealing true individuality. They are communal, and careful about what readers or other poets might think. They are painfully self-conscious, and anxious to be and do the right thing."
— John Bayley, *Poetry Review*

"He was viciously Stalinist, masculinist, pugilistic in a way that was good then but isn't now, and I would have died from his cigarette smoke. None of that confiscates his genius."
— Robert Crawford, on Hugh MacDiarmid, *Oxford Poetry*

"I do not give the honorific name of 'poetry' to the primitive and the unaccomplished."
— Helen Vendler, *New York Times*

"The wobble and flop of (William) McGonagall is the signature of his genius."
— Seamus Heaney, *The Times*

Poets as Nomads:

"The figure of the poet as 20th century jetlagged nomad is gaining ground."
— Helen Dunmore, *Poetry Review*

"It's crazy, all this travelling people go in for... If you stay put, you can travel in your imagination."
— George Mackay Brown, *The Sunday Telegraph*

"It is the business of poets to be neither here nor there."
— Alan Coren, *The Times*

"Only poetry recognises and maintains the centrality of absolutely everywhere."
— Les Murray, *Krino*

"Poetry can actually bring separate worlds together. You weave it together and it makes a sweater."
— Nikki Giovanni, *AWP Chronicle*

"The materials of physical composition aside, there is nothing a writer needs but a view out of a window... Writers, or more specifically poets, are not created by travel, exile or exotica, nor by personal trauma or substance abuse."
— Glyn Maxwell, *Critical Survey*

"The first-line test is a good one: has the poet seized an irresistible momentum from the flux of experience and language, or is he merely looking out the window, telling you it's a nice day, and casting round for a subject?"
— Edna Longley, *Krino*

On The Standing Armies:

"There are many more poets in this country than Kavanagh might have guessed."
— Fred Johnston, *Books Ireland*

"It appears that the number of active poetry readers and writers in Britain lies between 5,000 and 20,000; ... 0.01 — 0.03 per cent of the 56 million population."
— Roy Blackman, researcher, *Agenda*

"Last year's edition of the *Directory of American Poets* included 4,672 poets, all of them published, and all of them, incredibly, approved by a committee which determines that they are, in fact, poets. To read only one book by every living American poet — at the rate of one book a day, with no weekends or holidays off— would take thirteen years, during which time another few thousand poets would have appeared."
— Eliot Weinberger, *Index on Censorship*

As the poet said

The Last word:

"Poetry cannot be defined, only experienced."
— Christopher Logue, *Oxford Poetry*

Index

As the poet said